NUTSHELLS

ENVIRONMENTAL LAW

IN A

NUTSHELL

Other Titles in the Series

A Level Law
Company Law
Consumer Law
Contract Law
Constitutional and
Administrative Law
Criminal Law
Employment Law
English Legal System
European Union Law
Equity and Trusts
Evidence
Family Law
Human Rights
Intellectual Property Law
Land Law
Medical Law
Tort
Trusts

Titles in the Nutcase Series

Constitutional and
Administrative Law
Contract Law
Criminal Law
European Union Law
Employment Law
Equity and Trusts
Human Rights
Land Law
Tort

AUSTRALIA
Law Book Company
Sydney

CANADA and USA
Carswell
Toronto

HONG KONG
Sweet & Maxwell Asia

NEW ZEALAND
Brookers
Wellington

SINGAPORE and MALAYSIA
Sweet & Maxwell Asia
Singapore and Kuala Lumpur

NUTSHELLS

ENVIRONMENTAL LAW IN A NUTSHELL

FIRST EDITION

by

BRENDA SHORT, LL.B. (Hons), LL.M.
Visiting Lecturer, School of Law,
Southampton Institute

London ● Sweet & Maxwell ● 2004

Published in 2004 by Sweet & Maxwell Limited of
100 Avenue Road, London NW3 3PF
Typeset by J&L Composition, Filey, North Yorkshire
Printed and bound in Great Britain by Creative Print and Design
(Wales) Ebbw Vale

No natural forests were destroyed to make this product.
Only farmed timber was used and re-planted.

A CIP catalogue record for this book is available
from the British Library.

ISBN 0 421 797 908

CONTENTS

ABBREVIATIONS

Att-Gen	Attorney-General
AONB	Area of Outstanding Beauty
BAT	Best Available Techniques
BATNEEC	Best Available Techniques Not Exceeding Excessive Cost
BC	Borough Council
BPEO	Best Practicable Environmental Option
BPM	Best Practicable Means
CC	City Council or County Council
CAA 1993	Clean Air Act 1993
COPA 1974	Control of Pollution Act 1974
CPS	Crown Prosecution Service
DC	District Council
DEFRA	Dept. of Environment Food and Rural Affairs
DETR	former Dept of Environment, Transport and the Regions
DTLR	former Dept. of Transport, Local Govt. and the Regions
EEC	former European Economic Community
EC	European Community (see also EU)
ECHR	European Court of Human Rights
EJC	European Court of Justice
EIA	Environmental Impact Assessment
EMF	Electromagnetic Fields
EPA 1990	Environmental Protection Act 1990
EU	European Union (also see EC)
Ex p.	*Ex parte*
FoE	Friends of the Earth
HRA 1998	Human Rights Act 1998
HMIP	former Her Majesty's Inspectorate of Pollution
HSE	Health and Safety Executive
IPC	Integrated Pollution Control
IPPC	Interpreted Pollution Prevention and Control
LA	Local Authority
LBC	London Borough Council

LPA	Local Planning Authority
MBC	Metropolitan Borough Council
NRA	former National Rivers Authority
OCED	Organisation for Economic Co-operation and Development
ODPM	Office of Deputy Prime Minister
PACA 1991	Planning and Compensation Act 1991
PPC	Pollution Prevention and Control
PPCA 1999	Pollution Prevention and Control Act 1999
PPW	Packaging and Packaging Waste Directive
R. v F	*Rylands v Fletcher*
RCEP	Royal Commission for Environmental Pollution
SEA 1986	Single European Act 1986
TCPA 1990	Town and Country Planning Act 1990
TEU	Treaty of European Union (Maastricht Treaty)
UN	United Nations

INTRODUCTION

This book explains how the law can be used to protect the environment, the complex issues involved in environmental law and the relationship between law, policy and science. It introduces the legal framework used to regulate land use and pollution control together with the obligations it places on potential polluters. It also incorporates issues affecting the development of environmental law, the precautionary principle, enforcement of legislation by statutory bodies, Human Rights Act 1998, a citizen's right to legal redress including judicial review.

The law refers to the English Legal System which applies to England and Wales. However, devolved powers were acquired by Wales in 1999 and the Welsh Assembly is now able to introduce some legislation itself. Increasingly, environmental law within the UK has been derived from EU legislation and therefore, some laws apply to Scotland and Northern Ireland. Readers interested in the law in Scotland or Northern Ireland, should check whether particular legalisation applies to these countries.

---

1. ENGLISH LEGAL SYSTEM

This chapter introduces the basic principles of the English legal system to aid non lawyers. Law has a language of its own, some legal terms are in Latin, and those wanting to learn more, may wish to use a Law Dictionary.

SOURCES OF LAW

Law is derived from common law, equity and legislation. Common law is based on cases heard in the courts and equity being the rules of fairness and natural justice which supplement common law. Equity evolved through a separate court system until late 19th century when it was integrated with the Common Law Courts which themselves have been superseded by the current court system. Common laws are not covered by Acts (statutes), although new legislation can supersede common law.

Legislation refers to the Laws passed by Parliament in an Act (also called Statute). New Legislation is introduced to change current law, consolidate or codify existing law, or introduce law to situations not covered by existing law. Legislation may be introduced after an inquiry or Government sponsored report. The Royal Commission on Environmental Pollution is an independent body which issues advisory reports on environmental issues for the Government to consider prior to developing new environmental legislation.

Classification of Law

Law can be classified as either:

1. Common Law or Statute Law

- **Common law** — developed from previous cases and custom and practice. Includes both civil and criminal law.
- **Statute Law** — from Acts passed by Parliament. Includes civil and criminal laws.

2. Civil Law or Criminal Law

- **Civil law** — Includes torts which are civil wrongs (nuisance, negligence, trespass), contract, property law, etc. A party to the action, can sue for an appropriate remedy. *e.g.* damages, injunction, etc. Civil law can be either common law or statute law.
- **Criminal Law** — Contravening a criminal law is a criminal offence and on conviction the defendant is given a punishment, *e.g.* fine, prison sentence, probation, etc). Criminal law can be either common law or statute law.

Common (Case) Law

Common law is when the law is developed by court cases. The English Legal system is one of the few legal systems to operate **Judicial Precedent**. The Doctrine of Judicial precedent, **Stare Decisis** – let the decision stand, means that once a decision is made in a case, other judges will be bound to follow that decision in similar cases. Only cases heard in the higher courts are able to give precedent. The **Ratio Decidendi** is the legal reason the judge makes his decision. The **ratio decidendi** is the **binding precedent** and must be followed. Not all judges create a precedent, only where new principles of law are formed, will the decision create a precedent. The Judge may also make a 'helpful remark', and this is known as **Obiter Dicta**. It is not binding, but is a **Persuasive Precedent**. If the Judge is dealing with case where the law has been unclear, he might consider what the decision would have been if the situation had been slightly different, thus giving guidance to other courts.

Ways to avoid precedent:

- Court not bound by a decision in a lower ranking court. Therefore if it disagrees with previous decision, may **Overrule it.**
- A judge may **distinguish** the case he is deciding as being different from the previous case where the precedent was decided, thus avoid using it as precedent.
- Judge may rule that a previous decision was made **Per incurian** (by mistake).
- It is **Overturned** by a higher court.

Court Hierarchy Relating to Judicial Precedent

European Court of Justice decides matters of EU law that are then binding on English Courts.

House of Lords is not bound by its own decisions since House of Lords Practice Statement 1966.

Court of Appeal Criminal Division Following *R v Simpson* (2003), this court has discretion over whether a previous decision should be treated as binding precedent. The Court of Appeal binds all inferior (lower) courts.

Court of Appeal (Civil Division) normally bound by its own previous decisions unless decision over-ruled by House of Lords. Binds all inferior (lower) courts.

High Court – Appellate Division will bind courts of first instance of the High Court and all inferior courts. It is bound by its own decisions.

First Instance Courts: High Courts, County Courts, Crown Courts & Magistrates Courts The court where a case commences is called *Court of First Instance*. Decisions made by *Courts of First Instance* do not bind courts of the same status. This applies to High Court, Crown Court, County Court and Magistrates Court. The County Court and Magistrates Court have no power to bind another court at all.

Law reports give an account of a court case and the reasons for the judgment. Not all cases are reported, only the more important cases and ones which create new precedent. When a case is cited, details are given of the law report(s) where the case is reported. *E.g.* *Cambridge Water Co v Eastern Counties Leather Plc* (1994) 1 All E.R. 53, refers to All England Law Reports for 1994, Volume 1, page 53. Abbreviations for law reports can be found in a law dictionary.

Statute Law

Statute Law is primary legislation as it is passed by Parliament in an Act (Statute). It is generally superior to all other sources of law and enforced by judges through the courts system. Only EU law takes priority over English law if there is a conflict of laws.

English law also has to comply with the Human Rights Act 1998. The UK is a party to the European Convention of Human Rights and 1998 Act brought this convention into domestic law. Prior to the new legislation, any challenges relating to the infringement of human rights had to be taken to the European Court of Human Rights (includes the European Commission of Human Rights) at Strasbourg. (ECHR should not be confused with the European Courts of Justice (EJC) which is part of European Union). The HRA 1998 came into force in 2000 and the Convention is now directly applicable to all areas of domestic law which have to be compatible with the Act.

A **Statutory Instrument** (also known as Regulation or Order) is secondary legislation and is usually introduced without being debated in Parliament. Increasingly, Parliament is introducing 'enabling Acts' which allow the Government Department to introduce amendments or updates in the law through statutory instruments without going back to Parliament for new authority.

Statutory Interpretation:

When a judge is considering a case and needs to decides how to interpret a word in an Act (statute), he will consider the following rules:

- **Literal Rule** means taking the literal meaning of the words.
- **Golden Rule** can be used if the literal rule produces an absurd result, the judge can look further and ascertain the intention of parliament.
- **Mischief Rule** When words in the Statute are not clear in a literal sense, it is permissible to consider: What the common law was before Act, the defect for which common law did not provide a remedy, the reason Parliament decided on the remedy
- **Purposive approach** is becoming more common; it looks beyond the statute for the reasons for the Act. Since *Pepper v Hart* (1993), the judge can now look at Hansard Reports to see Parliament's intentions.
- **Ejusdem Generis Rule** means of the same kind
- **Expressio unios est exclusio alterius** the express mention of one thing, excludes another.

STRUCTURE OF THE COURTS

There is a separate court structure for ciminal and civil courts. However, some courts have jurisdiction in both civil and criminal matters — House of Lords, Court of Appeal, High Court and Magistrates Court.

Criminal Courts

The Crown Prosecution Service (CPS) was formed in 1985 and it now handles the prosecution of cases instead of the Police. When deciding whether to proceed with a case, the CPS have to consider the weight of evidence and the prospect of conviction. With environmental crimes, regulatory bodies are authorised to take prosecutions, *e.g.* Environment Agency, Health and Safety Executive and Local Authority. Customs and Excise deal with illegal import of endangered species. Anyone may take a private criminal prosecution unless the Statute restricts who may take a prosecution, *R. v Stewart* (1896).

In criminal cases, the party taking the criminal prosecution is called the prosecutor and the person being tried for the offence is called the defendant. If the defendant is convicted (found guilty), he will receive a punishment, *e.g.* fine, community sentences, imprisonment.

The Magistrates Court (with regard to Criminal cases)

As a Court of Inquiry, it investigates to see if there is a case to answer. Depending on the type of case, will decide the outcome or transfer it on to a higher court. Criminal cases can be suitable for:

- Summary trial in the magistrates court,
- Indictable — triable in the crown court, or
- 'Either way' being suitable for summary trial or indictable, depending on the circumstances of the particular case.

Cases are tried by magistrates, who are advised by the Clerk to the Court.

- **Lay Magistrates** are unpaid volunteers, recruited by the Department of Consitutional Affairs, formerly the Lord Chancellor's Office and trained to administer the law. Three lay magistrates normally 'sit' together and make joint decisions, with the more senior magistrate being the 'chair' and spokesman.
- **A Stipendiary Magistrate** is an experienced lawyer who is employed by the Court Service. He sits alone and is often appointed in areas where it is difficult to recruit lay magistrates. A stipendiary magistrate is now called a **District Judge.**
- **The Clerk to the Court**, employed by the Court Service, is legally qualified.

Magistrates Courts have limited sentencing powers. The maximum sentencing power for any one crime is currently a maximum custodial sentence of up to 6 months (with a maximum of 12 months for 2 or more consecutive offences) and/or fine. These sentencing powers may be extended when the Criminal Justice Bill becomes law. If the magistrates court feels its powers of sentencing are insufficient in a particular case, it can send the case up to Crown Court for sentencing.

Crown Court (only deals with criminal cases)

It has High Court status. High Court Judge sits as the arbitrator of law and 12 lay jurors are the arbitrators of fact and decide if defendant guilty or innocent. Jurisdiction:

- It deals with trials of indictable or either way offences,
- Commitals for sentencing from the Magistrates Court; and
- Appeals from magistrates courts against sentence and conviction.

The Divisional Courts of the High Court (criminal cases from magistrates court) The Divisional Court of the Queens Bench Division hears appeals by way of case stated from magistrates court. Appeals can be made by either the prosecutor or defendant only if they consider that the magistrates court was wrong in law or acted in excess of its jurisdiction. Other appeals from the magistrates court are heard in the Crown Court.

Court of Appeal — Criminal Division The Court of Appeal hears appeals from the Crown Court:

- By defendant against conviction and sentence.
- Application for review of sentence if too lenient.
- By mixed questions of fact and law.

House of Lords (Criminal cases) Hears appeals from High Court ('leapfrog' appeals) or Court of Appeal, Criminal Division, provided an inferior court certificates that a point of public importance is involved and it believes the point of law worthy of consideration. Normally 5 law lords sit on a case. A House of Lords decision, whether unanimous or a majority decision, is binding on all lower courts. Appeal cases need permission (previously called leave) of the Courts.

Civil Courts

In civil litigation, the party taking the court action is called the claimant (previously called the plaintiff). The person being sued is called the defendant. If the claimant's action against the defendant is successful, the judge will award a remedy, *e.g.* damages, injunction.

Magistrates — (with regard to civil cases) Apart from criminal cases, the magistrates, hear some domestic proceedings, issue licenses for public houses, some administrative law. Administrative law relates to the powers and duties of public bodies.

County Court (hears civil cases only) A district judge presides over day to day administration of courts. The County Court hear actions in tort and contract, personal injury, etc. Whether a case is taken in county or high court, depends on the amount of damages claimed and the complexity of claim.

High Court (civil cases)   It mainly sits in London. High Court judges normally sit in one of the divisions.

- **Queens Bench Division** Mainly contract and tort cases (cases unsuitable for county court, *e.g.* high amount of damages claimed). Admiralty, Commercial and Administrative Court.
- **Divisional Court of Queens Bench Division** Hears appeals from Magistrates Court and Crown Court 'by way of case stated' and judicial reviews.
- **Family Division** and **Divisional Court of Family Division**
- **Chancery Division** and **Div. Court of Chancery Division**

Court of Appeal — Civil Division   It is headed by the Master of the Rolls & Lord Justices of Appeal. Normally 3 Judges sit and hear appeals on matter of fact and law from: High Court, County Court, Various tribunals.

House of Lords (in relation to civil cases)   It is headed by the Lord Chancellor (now known as the Secretary of State for Consitutional Affairs and the Lord Chancellor). Normally 5 law lords sit and the Court hears civil case appeals from:

- Division Court of QBD provided: Inferior court certificates that a point of public important is involved and it believes point of law worthy of consideration
- Court of Appeal (civil division)
- High Court where leapfrog procedure operates.

A House of Lords decision, whether unanimous or majority decision, is binding on all lower courts.

Appeal cases usually need permission of the court for an appeal to be heard. Decisions in appeal cases do not have to be unanimous. When a Court of Appeal/House of Lords case is decided, at least one judge will give a detailed judgment giving the reason for the decision. The other judges may also make detailed judgments; on occasion they may agree with the decision, but give different reasons for coming to that decision in their judgment. If the judges are not agreed on the decision, the case will be decided on the majority decision. The judgment of judge(s) with the minority decision is known as a 'dissenting' judgment(s).

OTHER COURTS/WAYS OF REDRESS

European Court of Justice (ECJ)   If a court or tribunal considers that a case may be affected by EU law, but needs the law to be clarified before it can make a decision, it can apply to the ECJ. Under Art.234 (ex Art.177) of the EC Treaty, domestic courts of member states can refer to the ECJ for a preliminary ruling of EU law concerning the interpretation of the treaty, the validity and interpretation of acts of the institutions of the Community and the interpretation of the statutes of bodies established by an act of the Council, where those statutes provide.

Tribunals   May be used for the resolution of some disputes rather than the courts. Jurisdiction laid down by the Act of Parliament that creates the tribunal.

Alternative Dispute Resolution   ADR covers a range of alternatives for dispute resolution other than courts and tribunals.

Ombudsman

The Parliamentary Commissioner for Administration (referred to as the Ombudsman) and the can be asked to investigate when Government or Department fails to perform its duties to an appropriate standard and it is not a matter that can be challenged in the courts. Once the 'aggrieved person' has exhausted all other avenues of complaint, he can ask the Ombudsman to investigate maladministration. An ombudsman can only make recommendations and has no statutory power to award damages or overturn a decision. There is a Commissioner for Local Government (Local Government Ombudsman) but no Ombudsman for regulatory public bodies such as Environment Agency or English Nature.

JUDICIAL REVIEW — CHALLENGES ACTIONS OF PUBLIC BODIES

This is a matter of public law rather than private law. An individual can challenge the a decision that was made by a court, tribunal, Government or public body. Judicial review is provided for in The Rules of the Supreme Court, Ord. 53, now found in Civil Procedure Rules 1998. A Judge decides whether the body

has acted appropriately in exercising its public duty rather than reviewing the decision itself.
An application is two fold.

1) The judge will decide whether the applicant has 'standing' (also called *locus standi*). 'Standing' is where the individual (or organisation) demonstrates he has 'sufficient interest' in the case to be allowed to make a challenge.
2) If the applicant is able to prove 'standing', the case proceeds to a full hearing where the merits of the case are considered.

Applicants can succeed in their appeal for a judicial review to be heard, but the challenge has failed at the full hearing. Other applicants have felt they had a very strong challenge, which was likely to succeed, but have failed to be allowed a full hearing as they did not have 'standing'.

Grounds for review:

- **Illegality/Ultra Vires** this is when a body acts beyond its powers.
- **Irrationality** (or 'Wednesbury' Unreasonableness, see *Associated Picture Houses Ltd v Wednesbury Corporation* (1948))
- **Procedural impropriety** Failure to comply with legislative procedures.
- **Rules of Natural justice** No person to be condemned with out a hearing, No person to be a judge in his own cause, Legitimate expectation.

Remedies

- **Certiorari** — quashing a decision.
- **Prohibition** — forbidding a proposed course of action.
- **Mandamus** — ordering something to be done.
- **Declaration** — court decides and declares what the law is.
- **Injunction** — person is required to act or refrain from an act.
- **Discovery** — party has to disclose documents in their possession.
- **Damages** — compensation for loss suffered.

Legal Costs and Funding

Those facing criminal charges and on a low income, may be entitled to public funding through the Criminal Legal Service. Those who have insufficient means to pay for civil litigation can apply for public funding from the Community Legal Service (previously called legal aid). There is a two fold test: a) the case has merit and there is prospect of success and b) the applicant has to meet the financial criteria. Only those with disposable income and/or capital below certain amounts are eligible. The financial test takes into account the applicant's disposable income and capital, and capital in an applicant's main or only dwelling. The Woolf Reforms removed the right to public funding for some types of litigation and claimants now having to fund these cases through law firms offering Conditional Fee Agreements (CFA, also known as 'No Win No Fee' cases). The claimant may have to take out an 'after the event' insurance bond. Some firms will take 'No Win, No Fee' cases if the claimant buys an insurance bond. Individuals with 'Legal Expenses' Insurance may be able to make a claim on their policy.

In civil litigation, the party who loses the case may be ordered to pay the legal costs of the other party. This is often waived if the claimant is on a low income and has received public funding. During civil litigation, a defendant may make an offer which he pays into court, which the claimant can accept in settlement of the case. If the claimant refuses to accept the offer and subsequently wins the case but the court awards a lesser sum by the court, then the claimant will become liable for their own and the other party's costs from the time the payment was made.

---

2. WHAT CONSTITUTES ENVIRONMENTAL LAW?

The Environmental Protection Act 1990, defines the environment as: *'The 'Environment' consists of all, or any of the following media, namely, the air, water and land; and the medium of air includes the air within buildings and the air within other natural or man-made structures above or below ground'.*

Anti-pollution laws date from the 19th century, although environmental law as a body of law, has evolved over the latter part of the 20th century. Growing scientific knowledge has brought awareness of the need to protect to the environment, particularly from irreversible harm or damage. The need for environment protection ranges from global issues to localised problems. The UK Government is a signatory to a number of international conventions designed to protect the environment and the UK is a member of the European Union. Therefore, environmental law encompasses both International and EU law as well as domestic Law.

The 4 main principles enshrined in environmental law are: Preventative Principle, Polluter Pays, Precautionary Principle, Sustainable Development. Principles such as these, along with other environmental policies and aims are sometimes referred to as 'soft law'. In comparison, 'hard law' refers to actual laws which can be enforced.

Examples of Global pollution:

Depleted ozone layer, Climate changes, fall out from nuclear disaster (*e.g.*, Chernobyl Nuclear Power station disaster in 1986). Global problems are usually tackled at an international level.

Examples of Transboundary pollution:

Air, river and maritime pollution can all cross country borders.

Examples of Domestic pollution:

Water pollution, noise pollution, light pollution, visual pollution (can be minimized by planning laws), atmospheric pollution including radiation, contaminated land, dumping of waste materials (hazardous, non hazardous).

Examples of sources of pollution/environmental harm:

Factories, manufacturers, industries, businesses with waste products, mines, quarrying, power stations, power lines, mobile phone masts, planes, vehicles, built developments, schools, colleges, hospitals, domestic residences.

Environmental protection needed:

- To preserve environment.
- To create programme of sustainable development.
- To bring in controls to prevent pollution occurring.
- For a precautionary approach to be taken when there is scientific uncertainty as to whether irreversible harm is being caused to the environment.
- To control development of the land.

What laws can protect the environment:

- International treaties — incorporated in UK law.
- EU law — directives which have to be incorporated in domestic law and regulations which take direct effect.
- UK law (English legal system): criminal and civil law.

REGULATORS:

Examples of regulators:

- **The Environment Agency** became operational and assumed the existing functions of the National Rivers Authority (NRA), Her Majesty's Inspectorate of Pollution (HMIP) and Waste Regulatory Authorities (WRA) in 1996.
- **Health and Safety Executive**
- **Local Authority:** Environmental Health, Planning, Consumer Protection/Trading Standards.

Who can take a criminal prosecution:

Regulators can take a criminal prosecution and Environmental protection Laws often specify a regulatory body to oversee compliance of the law, including powers to prosecute offenders. (In certain circumstances the Government's Att-Gen can prosecute on behalf of Central Government *e.g.* Public Nuisance.) Pressure groups campaigns, class action, and individuals can also take a prosecution, anyone can unless 'statute barred', *i.e.* the Act restricts who can take a prosecution.

What courts?

Depending on the type of case, it will be heard in the English civil or criminal courts. Cases are occasionally referred to ECJ for a preliminary ruling on EU law. Some environmental cases involving human rights have been heard in ECHR, although since the introduction of the HRA 1998, domestic courts have had to take into account an individual's rights under the European Convention.

Cost of legal action, who pays?

The question of who pays the legal costs, depends on who is taking action and costs can be borne by:

- Regulator (*e.g.* Environment Agency).
- Central Government funds action by CPS or Att-Gen.
- Individual/ company privately funding case.
- Government funded legal help (the Community Legal Service).
- Insurance (*e.g* legal expenses policy).
- 'No win No fee' agreements with legal firms.

ENVIRONMENTAL LAWS

Environmental law includes both civil and criminal law. Much of the regulation of pollution and control of land use is classed as administrative law and dealt with through the civil courts. Contravening regulations can become a criminal offence, *e.g.* A person is not committing a criminal offence if he contravene planning regulations and is issued an enforcement notice by the local planning authority. However, it is a criminal offence to fail to comply with the conditions of the enforcement notice.

Examples of environmental law:

- Torts of (private) nuisance, negligence, trespass.
- Land Law.
- Town and Country Planning Legislation.
- Consumer Protection legislation.
- Public Health Legislation.
- Health and Safety at Work Legislation, including s.37 of the Health and Safety at Work, etc. Act 1974.
- Environmental Protection Statutes, *e.g.* Environmental Protection Act 1990, Water Resources Act 1991, Environment Act 1995, Pollution Prevention & Control Act 1999.

- Public nuisance.
- Manslaughter by gross criminal negligence.

Sources of environmental law:

- International treaties.
- EU Legislation.
- UK Primary legislation (Acts, also known as statutes).
- UK Secondary legislation (Statutory Instruments, also known as Regulations).
- Case law.
- Government Department Notes such as Planning Policy Guidance Notes.
- Government Circulars, Codes of Practice.
- Enforcement Authority Guidance Notes.

When deciding whether to take legal action, it is necessary to decide which law to use: civil action or a criminal prosecution. It depends on what outcome required: is it to prevent further pollution or is it an individual wanting personal redress, *e.g.* damages.

DIFFERENCES BETWEEN CIVIL LITIGATION & CRIMINAL PROSECUTION:

- **The standard of proof required** for civil cases is 'on balance of probabilities', in comparison it is much higher for a criminal case where it has to be 'beyond reasonable doubt'.
- **'Standing'.** In civil cases, the claimant has to prove 'standing', to show he is sufficiently affected by the defendant's actions to take action. With a private prosecution, anyone can prosecute, they do not have to be personally affected by the alleged offence.
- **Litigation Costs.** In civil action, the case has to be funded by the individual. Unless the claimant is on a very low income, he/she will not be funded by the Community Legal Service. Hence, environmental cases are sometimes brought by children as they are more likely to be eligible for public funding. Sometimes a group of campaigners will pool together a fighting fund to take civil action against a particular polluter or to take a 'test' case. In a criminal prosecution, a regulatory body will fund its

litigation. A private prosecutor can be awarded costs out of central funds at the end of the trial if directed by the court.

• **The outcome.** In civil action, the successful claimant will be granted a remedy, *e.g.* damages. In a criminal prosecution, the defendant is punished if found guilty of an offence.

Criminal law

A person is prosecuted through the criminal courts if they break a criminal law and commit an offence. A criminal law can be common law, *e.g.* public nuisance, or statute law. If someone dies as a result of pollution caused by human error, it is possible that the person(s) responsible could be prosecuted for manslaughter by gross criminal negligence. A prosecution for corporate manslaughter can be brought against a company whose actions have resulted in death, but very few cases have been taken. The larger the company, the more difficult it is to identify a senior member of the company whose negligent conduct could be attributed to the corporation. The Law Commission recommended a new offence of 'Corporate Killing' in 1996, but no new legislation has followed to date. Following the death of 4 passengers in the Hatfield train crash in 2000, in 2003 the CPS brought criminal charges of corporate manslaughter against Railtrack and Balfour Beauty and charges of manslaughter and offences under s.37 of the Health and Safety at Work Act 1974 against some individual managers. Similar charges could be brought against a company causing injury or death by severe environmental pollution.

If convicted of a criminal offence, an offender will be punished. In 2000, the *Sentencing Advisory Panel* issued advice to the Court of Appeal on sentencing guidelines for environmental offences. The Court of Appeal considered the Sentencing Advisory Panel's advice in *Milford Haven Port Authority ('The Sea Empress')* (2000), but decided not to issue sentencing guidelines for environmental offences on that occasion. *R. v F. Howe & sons Engineers) Ltd* (1999) gave guidance on sentencing and *R v Friskies Petcare UK Ltd* (2000) sets out guidelines for the sentencing court for guilty pleas. Fines for environmental offences depend on the actual offence committed, but they can be up to £20,000 in magistrates court and unlimited in Crown Court. In 2001, the Magistrates Association issued guidance sentencing in environmental cases, 'Fining companies for environmental and Health and Safety offences'. In

2002, the Magistrate's Association issued a comprehensive information toolkit on many aspects of environmental crime. It included 'Costing the Earth-Environmental Crime', guidance on sentencing for various environmental offences (see *www.magis trates-association.org.uk*). The guidelines suggest factors which should be taken into consideration when passing sentence, and stresses the importance of taking into account the risk of harm as well as actual harm caused. Guidelines on sentencing in Wildlife Trade and Conservation Offences were also issued. In passing sentence, the magistrates should reflect the seriousness of the crime and ensure that it is more costly to commit an offence than it is to comply with the law.

Civil Law

If a person has committed a civil wrong, action can be taken through the civil courts. If the claimant (previously called the plaintiff) is successful, then the courts will grant the claimant a remedy (*e.g.* damages, injunction). A regulatory body taking a prosecution under criminal law does not prevent an individual who has suffered personally from taking civil action to recover damages.

THE FUTURE

Increasingly, criminal offences are being introduced under Statute law in respect of pollution. Environmental law is also being progressively determined by EU law. As well as EU directives on specific areas of pollution, following a white paper on Environmental Liability in 2000, the commission has issued a draft directive to implement a polluter pays regime in respect of environmental damage. In 2003, the EU issued a Decision on the Protection of the Environment through Criminal Law, requiring member states to establish criminal offences for certain intentional acts and negligent acts . Both the UK and the EU are signatories to the 1998 Aarhus Convention which will allow more public participation in environmental decision making. In 1999, the Dept of Environment initiated a study to investigate the feasibility of establishing an environmental court (the report may still be available on *www.planning.odpm.gov.uk/court*). In 2003, DEFRA supported research projects into the case for environmental tribunals.

3. TOOLS OF THE ENVIRONMENTAL LAWYER

Individuals and public interest groups increasingly look to the law to help prevent pollution, environmental damage or development of land. If an individual is personally affected, he make take wish to take civil legal action in tort to remedy the situation, *e.g.* to obtain damages, injunction. Alternatively, he may wish to take a judicial review to challenge the actions of a public body who have acted illegally or with flawed decision making. When deciding what action to take, it is necessary to take into account litigation costs and desired outcome. If the person is not seeking damages, then it might be cheaper to consider other options, *e.g.* rather than a civil action in (private) nuisance, take action under statutory nuisance, s.82 of the EPA 1990.

CHECK LIST OF CIVIL ACTION:

- **Public nuisance** (is a tort as well as a crime).
- **Torts:** includes Negligence, Nuisance (private), *Rylands v Fletcher*, Trespass, Breach of Statutory Duty, Occupier's Liability.
- **Judicial review.**
- **Apply to EU for direct action under Art. 226 of EC Treaty.**

CHECK LIST OF CRIMINAL ACTION:

- **Statutory nuisance,** action can be taken by LA or individual.
- **Public Nuisance** (common law criminal offence)
- **Criminal Prosecution by regulator.**
- **Private Criminal Prosecution.**

Gradually, laws are being introduced which give the public increased access to information, rights of public participation and access to justice in environmental matters. Until then, their main courses of action will be challenging the decisions of a public body through judicial review, or private criminal prosecution if a regulator fails to act. A judicial review can be made on the grounds that the decision makers have not taken into account the possible risks of environmental harm or health risks in situations where there is scientific uncertainty. Campaigners may ask for a precautionary or prudent approach to be taken where there is scientific uncertainty (See the unsuccessful *Duddridge* case). Since the Human Rights Act 1998 incorporated the European Convention of Human Rights into domestic law, there has been an increase in the number of challenges on human rights grounds. EU decisions can be challenged by judicial review.

PUBLIC ACCESS TO INFORMATION/PUBLIC PARTICIPATION/ACCESS TO JUSTICE

Public access to information is a key factor for environmental campaigners and individuals who wish to take action over environmental pollution. It allows them to find out the answers to questions such as: does a company have authorisation for discharges? Are attached conditions being adhered to? There have been various policies and measures taken to give freedom of access to the public on environmental matters, allow public participation in the decision making process and give access to justice. These policies have been expressed at international, EU and national level.

International Law

The Rio Declaration (1992), Principle 10 states '*environmental issues are best handled with participation of concerned citizens, at the relevant level*'. The 1998 Aarhus Convention on Access to Information, Public Participation in Decision Making and Access to Justice in Environmental matters will increase Government accountability, remove environmental secrecy and increase the public's environmental rights, including the right to challenge public authorities and polluters who contravene regulations. The UN pan-European treaty came into force in 2001 and the EU and UK are preparing to ratify it.

EU Law

The EC's 5th Environmental Action Programme (agreed in 1992 and covering the period 1993-2000) stated '*Individuals and public interest groups should have practicable access to the courts in order to ensure that their legitimate interests are protected and that prescribed*

*environmental measures are effectively enforced and illegal practices
stopped'*. The EU is preparing to ratify the 1998, Aarhus
Convention. In 2002, the EU issued a working document for a
proposed Directive on Access to Justice in Environmental
Matters. It issued a further draft Directive on Public Access to
Environmental Information in 2003, which will replace the 1990
Directive on Freedom of Access to Information on the
Environment. The EU has adopted a proposal to introduce an
environmental liability regime aimed at environmental damage
as well as traditional damage (damage to goods and person).

National law

The UK RCEP's 10th report (1984) recommended the public have
access to environmental information. The 1990 EU Directive
Freedom of Access was introduced into UK law through
Environmental Information Regulations 1992. Every relevant
person who holds any information to which the regulations apply,
is under a duty to make information available to every person who
requests it, with certain exceptions. Some Statutes provide that
regulators must provide public information registers. The
Freedom of Information Act 2000 provides for improved access to
information held by public authorities about their responsibilities
and activities. DEFRA is supporting 3 research projects relating to
Access to Justice: examining the case for the establishing
environmental tribunals, analysing the English court system as a
tool of environmental justice and evaluating how effective access
to environmental justice is within England and Wales. The projects
are expected to report back in 2003. Another project is examining
the sentencing in environmental offences.

CRIMINAL ACTION

Statutory Nuisance

Under s.82 of the EPA 1990, if a Local Authority (LA) fails to take
action, an 'aggrieved person' is able to act in person and apply to
the Magistrates Court. (See chapter on Statutory Nuisance).

Public nuisance

Public Nuisance is a common law criminal offence and defined as
'an act, not warranted by law, materially affecting the reasonable

comfort of a class of her Majesty's subjects who come within the sphere or neighbourhood of its operation'. Whether the group of people affected by the nuisance are counted as a class, is a question of fact in each case. LAs, under s.222 of the Local Government Act 1972, and the Att-Gen have powers to prosecute under public nuisance. An individual can take an injunction with the consent of the Att-Gen (relator action).

South West Water was prosecuted in 1992 for public nuisance, following the *Camelford Water contamination* case. In *Gillingham BC v Medway (Chatham Dock Co)* (1993), after planning permission was given for a port, heavy traffic built up and LA brought an action in public nuisance and an injunction to restrain the traffic at night. The Court decided although traffic disturbed the residents, it was a lawful use of the highway. There was not actionable claim in nuisance based on the character of the neighbourhood since planning permission had been granted for the port. In *Wandsworth LBC v Railtrack Plc* (2001), the Court of Appeal upheld that an infestation of pigeons on a bridge interfered with the comfort and convenience of pedestrians and constituted a public nuisance which was the responsibility of the bridge owner.

Aggravated Trespass (a criminal offence)

As well as trespass being a tort in civil law, trespas can also be a criminal offence under Part V of Criminal Justice and Public Order Act 1994. Section 68 provides that a person commits the offence of aggravated trespass if he trespasses on land in the open air and intimidates, obstructs or disrupts a person who is lawfully engaged or about to engage in a lawful activity on that land or on an adjoining land. On summary conviction, the defendant is liable to a term of imprisonment not exceeding three months or a fine not exceeding level 4, or both. In *DPP v Tilly* (2001), the defendant appealed against her conviction in the magistrates court of aggravated trespass for damaging GM crops being grown for government sponsored trials. As the appeal was based on a point of law, it was heard in the High Court. The Court allowed the appeal on the grounds that there was not a person engaged in a relevant lawful activity present on the land at the time of the alleged trespass. If the person was absent, it was not possible to obstruct or disrupt them from engaging in a lawful activity.

Four protestors were charged with aggravated trespass aftger they chained themselves to a tractor during a demonstration against GM crops trials in 2002, but were acquitted in the magistrates court after they put forward a defence that they were acting to defend property. The DPP appealed to the High Court on a point of law as to whether the defence should have been accepted. The Court held that the district judge had erred in law by accepting their defence, which should only be allowed against an unlawful or criminal act and GM trials were being conducted lawfully, *DPP v Bayer* (2003).

Private criminal prosecution

Unless statute barred, anyone can take a private criminal prosecution, *R v Stewart* (1896), and this allows an individual to take action if the regulator fails to do so, A criminal prosecution can include statutes and common law. The FoE was considering a private prosecution in relation to the Sea Empress tanker disaster. The Environment Agency eventually took action and the Port Authority were fined £4 million, later reduced to £750,000 on appeal, *Environment Agency v Milford Haven Port Authority (Sea Empress)* (2000). In *Coghill v Morgan* (1998), the magistrates court allowed a scientist to take a private criminal prosecution against a mobile phone shop, based on the authority of *R. v Stewart* (1896).

Future Legislation

In 2003 the EU made a Framework Decision on the Protection of the Environment through Crime, requiring member states to bring environmental pollution under criminal law. The UK has already adopted criminal law to protect the environment, through its regulatory regimes.

CIVIL ACTION

Human Rights and Human Rights Act 1998 (HRA 1998)

The HRA 1998 came into force on October, 2 2000 and incorporates into UK law, certain rights and freedoms contained in the European Convention on Human Rights. The Act applies to public authorities, who must ensure their actions do not breach an individual's human rights. Public Authorities are bodies undertaking functions of a public nature, *e.g.* government departments, LAs, courts, tribunals, regulatory bodies such as the Environment Agency and the Health & Safety Executive. In the case of proceedings against a public authority there is a limitation period of a year from the date of the act complained about. Many of the Articles do allow rights to be breached in certain circumstances. *E.g.* interests of national security, public safety. Arts 6, 8, and Art.1 of 1st protocol are the most likely to have the greatest impact on planning and environmental law.

The Convention of Human Rights includes:

Art.6 Right to a fair trial
1) *'In the determination of his civil rights and obligations or of any criminal charge against him, everyone is entitled to a fair and public hearing within a reasonable time by an independent and impartial tribunal established by law.'*
Art.8 Right to respect for private and family life
1) *'Everyone has the right to respect for his private and family life, his home and his correspondence'.*
2) *'There shall be no interference by a public authority with the exercise of this right except such as is in accordance with the law and is necessary in a democratic society in the interests of national security, public safety or the economic well-being of the country, for the prevention of disorder or crime, for the protection of health or morals, or for the protection of the rights and freedoms of others'.*
Art.13 Everyone whose rights under the Convention are violated shall have an effective remedy before a national authority.
Art.14 Prohibition of discrimination
Art.17 Prohibition of abuse of rights
Art.18 Limitation on use of restrictions on rights
The First Protocol, Art.1 – Protection of property
'Every natural or legal person is entitled to the peaceful enjoyment of his possessions. No one shall be deprived of his possessions except in the public interest and subject to the conditions provided for by law and by the general principles of international law'.
The First Protocol, Art.2, Right to education
Environmental campaigners and individuals have already used human rights law to challenge the actions of public bodies, mainly in connection with environmental/planning cases, so far with limited success (a number of cases are reported in the chapter on Planning).
Possible applications:

- refusal / withdrawal of legal aid. In *Secretary of State for ETR, Ex p. Challenger* (2000), the applicants applied for a review of the decision not to provide legal assistance for local objectors, breaching Art.6 right to fair trial. The court was unable to allow a judicial review as the Act had not come into force.

- decision of planning authority to the siting of a hazardous operation near to residential area, *e.g. R. (Vetterlein) v Hampshire CC* (2001).
- failure of Regulator to take enforcement action.
- government bodies failing to provide adequate information to local residents about the health risks posed by a hazardous operation in their area.
- challenging various laws as being incompatible with the HRA.
- A number of planning cases have been challenged on the grounds that the applicant was denied the right to a fair trial under Art.6.

Before the HRA 1998 came into force in October. 2000, cases had to be taken before the European Court of Human Rights (ECHR). Campaigners affected by the noise from night flights at Heathrow, took an unsuccessful judicial review in the English courts against the Government's decision to allow night flights. The campaigners then appealed to ECHR, stating that the UK Government had violated their rights under Art.8 and Art.13. The ECHR made an interim judgment in favour of the applicants. The final judgment held there had been no violation of Art.8 but their rights to an effective remedy before a national court under Art.13 had been violated, and subsequently they were awarded damages, *Hatton v UK Government* (ECHR) (2003). Some early cases before the English courts failed as they were brought before the Act was introduced, including *Anscomb v Secretary of State for ETR* (2001) where a planning decision was made before the Act came into force.

The Court of Appeal allowed an appeal by landowners against a Parochial Church Council on the grounds that the church tax on glebe land infringed their human rights under Art.1 of 1st protocol, and Art.14, *Wallbank v PCC of Aston Cantlow* (2001). However, in 2003, the House of Lords allowed an appeal by PPC, on the grounds that it was not a core public authority under Art. 6, and the HRA 1998 did not apply. In *R v Hertfordshire CC Ex p. Green Environmental Industries* (2000), the House of Lords rejected an applicant's submission that Art.6 prevented self incrimination, holding that Art.6(1) was concerned with the fairness of a trial and not with extra judicial inquiries.

The High Court held that a sewerage undertaker had infringed a property owner' rights under Art.1 of 1st protocol in *Marcic v Thames Water* (2002), by failing to remedy flooding of their sewer system onto the property of Marcic. Thames Water appealed, and Marcic cross appealed against the dismissal of his claim in nuisance. The Court of Appeal held that the High Court had been correct to conclude that Thames Water had infringed the claimants rights under the 1998 Act. Any right that the claimant had to damages under that Act was, however, displaced by his common law right to damages. Contrary to the High Court Judge's finding, the claimant had a valid claim in nuisance.

JUDICIAL REVIEW

Judicial Review enables interest parties, such as individuals/ campaign groups, to challenge the actions or inaction of a government body. The applicant first has to prove that he has *locus standi* (or 'Standing') before being allowed a full hearing. The rules on 'standing' were established in *Inland Revenue v FSESB Ltd* (1982) and the known merits of the case have to be taken into account when deciding whether the applicant has 'sufficient interest' to proceed to a full hearing. In the past there has been a restrictive approach to 'standing'; often environmental campaign groups had been able to show public interest but not necessarily sufficient personal interest. This approach seems to have been relaxed in more recent cases, particularly judicial review challenges by established environmental groups, such as Friends of the Earth (FoE) and Greenpeace. The advantages of allowing 'standing' to the larger organisations is that they have the scientific and legal expertise, and funds, to mount a more focused and relevant challenge on public law issues. Local action groups are beginning to mount claims in the names of their children, as they are more likely to qualify for public funding. There is a short time limit for making an application and delay may now be more of a crucial factor than 'standing'. Judicial reviews normally have to be heard in 3 months although pending on the circumstances that may be considered too lengthy a delay, alternatively the court may allow a case to be heard 'out of time'.

Locus Standi

In *R. v Secretary of State for the Environment Ex p. Rose Theatre Trust* (1990) standing was refused to group of interested parties who formed a trust company to save the Elizabethan theatre. In *R v Poole BC Ex p. BEEBEE*(1991), a claim for a judicial review was made by BHS, a local conservation group, and World Wide Fund for Nature (WWF), regarding a grant of planning permission for a housing development on a Site of Special Scientific Interest (SSSI). The court stated if the case had not been brought with the consent of the respondent, then only BHS would have been given standing.

The RSPB were granted standing in *R. v Swale BC & Medway Ports Ex p. RSPB* (1991) as they had a legitimate expectation to be consulted before a planning decision was made and local authority had failed to consult them. Even though they did not have any personal interest in the case, the World Development Movement Ltd were granted 'standing' in *R. v Secretary of State of Foreign Affairs Ex p. WDM* (1995), to challenge the Government's decision to grant aid to Pergau Dam project. The late Andrew Lees, who was Campaign Director of FoE, was granted 'standing' to challenge the drinking water standard in his home area, in *R. v Secretary of State for Environment Ex p. FoE and Andrew Lees* (1994). The Secretary of State had decided to accept undertakings from Water Companies in breach of the EU Drinking Water Directive rather than take enforcement action and as Lees was resident in one of the relevant water authority areas, he was directly affected by the decision. In *R v Secretary of State of Trade & Industry Ex p. Duddridge & Others* (1994), local children were given 'standing' in their application to challenge the decision by the Dept of Trade & Industry to allow underground electricity cables to be laid near their homes.

In *R. v Secretary of State for the Environment Ex p. Greenpeace* (1994), Greenpeace and the local authority challenged decision by the Department of Environment and HMIP to allow a company to reprocess radioactive waste without a local inquiry. In *R. v HMIP Ex p. Greenpeace No.2* (1994), Greenpeace challenged the decision of HMIP to allow a reprocessing plant at Sellafield. In granting 'standing', the court took into account of the health interests of 2500 Greenpeace supporters in the region, Greenpeace was an established group campaigning for the protection of the environment and was accredited by UN and other international bodies. FoE and Greenpeace have been granted 'standing' in other cases, such as *R.(FoE and Greenpeace) v Secretary of State for EFRA* (2001), in a challenge to the Secretary of State's decision to allow Mixed Oxide Fuel at Sellafield. In *R.(Greenpeace) v Secretary of State for EFRA* (2002), Greenpeace were granted a full hearing but the Court of Appeal dismissed their challenge regarding import of mahogany from Brazil.

Judical Reviews defeated by undue delay

In *R. v North Somerset DC Ex p. Garnett* (1997), two local residents and FoE applied for leave to challenge the grant of planning permission for quarrying in a council owned public park. The planning decision was made on July 31, 1996, the applicants instructed solicitors on September 20, and application for judicial review was made on October 24, 1996. Even though it was within 3 month time limit, the application was dismissed as there had been undue delay by the applicants in bringing the case. *R. (Kides) v South Cambridgeshire DC* (2001), involved an application for judicial review of a grant of planning permission. The application was refused on several grounds, including undue delay as it was made outside the three month limit and the applicant, a local resident, did not have 'standing' in the case.

Judicial Review of EU law

EU law can also be challenged through judicial review. Greenpeace and local residents were not granted *locus standi* in *Stitching Greenpeace Council (Greenpeace International) v EC* (1998), a Spanish case, involving EU approved grant aid for 2 power plants in Canary Islands. An application for judicial review made on the grounds that projects did not have an environmental impact assessment, violating EU Directive. The applicants included farmers, residents, 2 local environmental pressure groups and Greenpeace. To bring an action under Art.230 (ex Art.173) of the EC treaty, applicants have to show that the decision being challenged is either addressed to them, or to another person and of 'direct and individual concern to them'. Greenpeace were not granted standing nor were applicants who could not show they were affected more than other residents. This rule was relaxed in *Jego-Quere & Cie SA v Commission* (2002), as the court stated the number and position of others affected was not releveant.

EU – direction Action under Art.226 (ex. Art.169)

The European Commission will, but is not obliged, to follow up complaints it receives from individuals, pressure groups, concerning breaches of EU Environmental Law. (see chapter on EU law).

---

4. TORT

Torts are civil wrongs, developed through common law, which allow a person who has suffered interference or damage to either his property or his person by another, to seek redress by obtaining damages and/or an injunction or an abatement. More than one person may be considered liable, in which case they can be sued as joint tortfeasors and if the claim succeeds, the court will apportion liability. An employer is normally vicariously liable for the actions of an employee, although not usually liable for the actions of an independent contractor.

The House of Lords extended the requirement for foreseeability to nuisance and *R v F* in *Cambridge Water Co v ECL* (1994). In this case, Lord Goff discouraged the development of common law for environmental pollution as statute law is being introduced for pollution control.

Evidence required for Torts

As torts are civil cases, it is only necessary to prove the case on balance of probabilities. Courts find it much easier to deal with claims for environmental harm/ pollution caused by a one off incident where a person suffers immediate loss or harm and it is much easier to establish the chain of causation between the incident and the harm caused. It is more difficult for a claimant to succeed in respect of historic pollution, gradual pollution, pollution possibly caused by more than one polluter, pollution caused by the combined reaction of 2 or more components and cases where there is a delay between exposure to pollutant and onset of symptoms of ill-health or environmental harm.

Scientific Uncertainty

To succeed in legal action it is necessary to have evidence to support the claim. However, in cases where there is scientific uncertainty it is not always possible to provide that proof, particularly if proof can only be ascertained as a result of large scale scientific/medical study. Proceedings were commenced in 5 test cases, including *Studholme v NORWEB*, against electricity suppliers for negligence, claiming their ill health had been caused by power lines. An awaited 1997 US study failed to give conclusive evidence of any correlation between EMFs and incidence of cancer, this resulted in legal aid being withdrawn and the cases discontinued. New or recommenced proceedings may be initiated once additional evidence becomes available.

Time Limits

Section 2(a)–(c) Limitation Act 1980 imposes a time limit for actions in tort, normally 6 years from the date on which the cause of action actually accrued. For personal injury, this is reduced to 3 years from the date the person suffered the injury or the date the claimant first knew of the damage, whichever is the later.

General Defences to Torts

As well as specific defences to particular torts, there are general defences:

- **Contributory Negligence** Damages are reduced if the claimant was partly to blame for the damage done.
- *Volenti Non Fit Injuria* No act is actionable in tort, if the person voluntarily consents to the act.
- **Necessity** An invasion of private rights at the time of emergency can justified if the act was reasonable at the time.
- **Statutory Authority** A defence of statutory authority can be raised by a statutory undertaker whose actions are the result of carrying out an activity expressly authorised, or implied, by the Statute, with reasonable care.

NEGLIGENCE

Certain relationships give rise to a legal duty, so that if one party acts carelessly and causes the other party to suffer harm or loss, then the injured party may sue for damages. Action can be taken against the person causing harm or in certain circumstances action can be taken against a public body for failing in its duty of care. Negligence does not require a legal interest in the land. To prove negligence:

- the claimant has to prove the defendant owed him a duty of care,
- that the defendant breached that duty of care,
- the claimant suffered harm as a direct result of breach,
- that harm was foreseeable and damages claimed are not too remote,
- the defendant does not have a valid defence.

Who owes duty of care?

The House of Lords defined the *'neighbour principle'* in *Donoghue v Stevenson* (1932) as *'persons who are so closely and directly affected by my act that I ought reasonably to have them in my contemplation'*. Subsequent cases have developed 'duty of care' and it now requires foreseeability of damage and sufficient proximity of parties. If these conditions are fulfilled, it must still be just and reasonable for a duty to be imposed.

What is the standard required and was duty of care breached?

In examining the act or omission of the defendant, it is necessary to determine whether he acted with a standard of care as would be expected from a 'reasonable man'. If the defendant is carrying out duties in relation to his profession or a specialist job, then the duty of care is judged on the standard of his profession. If the defendant has not acted with the required amount of care, then he may be found to have breached his duty of care. A person complying with current accepted practices and existing knowledge is less likely to be found negligent. In a situation where there has been scientific uncertainty, the court might consider not only what the scientific knowledge was at the time, but also whether it was known that there might be risk of harm as yet not proven.

Was harm/damage as a direct result of the breach?

The claimant has to prove, on the balance of probabilities, that the harm or loss suffered was a direct result of the defendant's breach of duty. There has to be a direct chain of causation; if the damage is caused by an intervening act over which the defendant has no control, it make break the chain of events. The doctrine of *Res Ipsa Loquitor* (the thing speaks for itself) applies when at first instance there appears to be evidence of negligence, but it is difficult to prove the precise cause of the negligent act.

Was the harm suffered foreseeable/remoteness of damage?

The defendant is not liable for all damages, only the damages that were foreseeable by a reasonable man. It is sufficient for it to be foreseeable that an act or omission could result in damage, it is not necessary for the defendant to know the precise damage caused. The defendant is still liable if the claimant is exceptionally susceptible and suffers greater harm than the average person.

Is there a valid defence for negligence?

- Contributory negligence
- *Volenti Non Fit Injuria*
- *Ex Turpi Causa non oritur actio*—A person can not take action if the alleged wrong happens when he was engaged in unlawful act.

Remedy for Negligence: Damages

NUISANCE (PRIVATE NUISANCE)

Nuisance is not to be confused with public nuisance or statutory nuisance. A claim in (private) nuisance is based on unlawful interference with a person's use or enjoyment of land.

Who can sue (private) nuisance?

The claimant has to have a legal interest in the land where they are suffering from the nuisance, *i.e.* tenant, owner. *Khorasandjian v Bush* (1993) extended rights to others in a household. The law was restricted again, in *Hunter v Canary Wharf* (1997), when the House of Lords re-instated the view that private nuisance action can only be excised by those with rights to the land affected. A case before the ECHR, *Khatun v UK Government* (ECHR) (1998), concerned residents without a legal interest in their home. The court stated that Art.8(1) applied to all the applicants, *e.g.* children of property owners, but the case failed on other grounds. *McKenna v British Aluminium Ltd* (2002), involved a claim in nuisance. The court refused to strike out the claims of those with no proprietary interest in the land, prior to the final hearing. The child claimants were relying on rights under Art.8 and the court stated that they had an arguable case that the restrictions of the common law should be extended following HRA 1998. The case settled before trial, so the existing restrictions on nuisance will not be reviewed after all. However, in the light of the *Khatun* case, heard before the ECHR, it would seem that the child claimants would have been granted standing in (private) nuisance.

Consideration as to whether there are grounds for nuisance:

- Duration and frequency of interference. A temporary interference is less likely to constitute a nuisance.
- Locality. Grant of planning permission not automatically defence to nuisance, *Wheeler v Saunders* (1995).
- Nature of activity causing nuisance.
- Sensitivity of claimant.
- Intent of parties. In *Hollywood Silver Fox Farm Ltd v Emmett* (1936) the defendant was deemed to have caused a nuisance as he had deliberately and maliciously annoyed the plaintiff.
- Use of best practicable means (BPM) to reduce nuisance.

Action can be taken by an individual or a group of people. It is not necessary to prove nuisance is injurious to health to take action for private nuisance.

Who is liable?

The creator of the nuisance. In certain circumstances, the occupier and landlord may be held liable even if they did not create the nuisance. There is still an element of strict liability in nuisance, as the claimant does not have to prove negligence, but does have to prove foreseeability following the House of Lords decision in *Cambridge Water* Case (1994).

Unlawful interference with a person's use or enjoyment of land:

a) causing an encroachment on a neighbour's land (similar to trespass).

b) causing physical damage to a neighbour's land or building or works or vegetation upon it, *e.g. St Helens Smelting Co v Tipping* (1865), *Halsey v Esso Petroleum* (1961).

c) unduly interfering with a neighbour in the enjoyment of his land, *e.g.* discomfort and inconvenience from such things as dust, noise and smells, but no physical harm.

In *Walter v Self* (1851), it was held that the standard of inconvenience has to 'materially interfere with the ordinary physical comfort of human existence'. In *Wheeler v Saunders Ltd* (1995), the Court of Appeal held that a LPA had no power to permit a nuisance apart from permitting a change in the character of a neighbourhood and the nuisance was an inevitable result of the authorised use. In *Murdoch v Glacier Metal Co Ltd* (1998), the Court of Appeal upheld the trial judge's decision to take into account the standards of the average person and the character of the neighbourhood when deciding whether the noise was sufficiently serious to amount to a nuisance. In *Baxter v Camden LBC* (No.2) (1999), a tenant made a claim in nuisance against LA landlord in respect of inadequate soundproofing from her neighbours. The House of Lords dismissed the claim, as the neighbours were using their properties in a normal way and the LA had not authorised any nuisance.

Defences for nuisance:

- *Volenti no fit injuria.*
- **Prescription.** The acquisition of an easement over land by long term use.
- **Statutory Authority.**

In *Blackburn v ARC Ltd* (1998), the operators of a landfill site were sued in nuisance relating to litter, smells, gases and noise from the site. Their defence of statutory authority failed as it was not inevitable that the nuisance would result from authorised duties.

Remedies for nuisance: Abatement, injunction and damages

RULE IN *RYLANDS V FLETCHER (R. V F)*

In House of Lords case, *Rylands v Fletcher* (1868), the defendant's contractors had unknowingly, flooded the plaintiff's mineshafts and although the defendant had not been negligent, he was found liable. The Court held that '*A person who for his own purposes brings on to his land and collects and keeps there anything likely to do mischief if it escapes, must keep in it at his peril, and if he does not do so, is prima facie answerable for all the damage which is the natural consequence of its escape.*' On appeal to the House of Lords, the judges agreed with the previous judgment and added that it had to be non natural use of land.

The House of Lords marked an important development to *R. v F* in the case of *Cambridge Water Co v Eastern Countries Leather* (1994). In 1983, the borehole of a water company (CWC) was contaminated by chemicals from a tannery business over a mile away. It was thought that the chemical spillages had seeped into the ground and been carried to the borehole by underground water. At the time of the court hearing, chemicals were still seeping into CWC's land. CWC claims in negligence and nuisance were dismissed at trial due to lack of foreseeability and *R. v F* dismissed on the grounds that the storage of the chemicals was a natural use of defendant's land. CWC appealed to the Court of Appeal on *R. v F* only; the appeal was allowed, not on the grounds of *R. v F*, but on the rule of strict liability in nuisance. The Judge based his decision on *Ballard v Tomlinson* (1885) which decided that where the nuisance is an interference with a natural right of ownership, then liability is a strict one. The defendant, ECL, appealed to the House of Lords, who allowed the appeal, stating that foreseeability of harm of the relevant type by the defendant was a prerequisite of the recovery of damages both in nuisance and under the rule in *R. v F*. Leaving aside whether the chemicals were a non–natural use of land, the plaintiff could not establish that, in the circumstances, the pollution was foreseeable. At the time that the chemical spillages occurred, it was not reasonable or foreseeable that it would result in pollution to an aquifer some distance away. Following this case, it has been argued that *R. v F* is an extension of nuisance. Although ECL had avoided damages in private law claim by CWC, the Company was still subject to public law and were required by the NRA (now Environment Agency) to carry out certain works to clean up the water pollution under Water Resources Act 1991.

Defences to *R. v F*: Statutory authority, Contributory

negligence, Necessity, Act of God, Common benefit, Independent act of 3rd party.

Remedies for R. v F: Damages, Injunction

TRESPASS

[The Tort of trespass is not to be confused with criminal offences of trespass and aggravated trespass under Part V of the Criminal Justice and Public Order Act 1994]. The advantage of trespass is that action can be taken even if no harm is caused. Trespass does not have to prove the defendant was negligent. Trespass to the person or to land is a direct interference of a person's personal or proprietary rights. Anyone who enters the land of another and is not a lawful visitor is a trespasser. A lawful visitor acting outside his rights, can become a trespasser. Trespass can also take the form of placing an object on the land or objects that touch the property, *e.g.* dumping rubbish on another's land. A claimant has to have possession of the land to take action. LACS was successful in its action in trespass on their unfenced land on Exmoor, used as a deer sanctuary, to hinder deer hunting, in *LACS v Scott* (1985). The court allowed an injunction in respect of an area where there had been trespass by the hunt on a number of occasions. The court stated that the Master of the Hunt allowing hunting close to the prohibited land, in circumstances which would make it effectively impossible to prevent the trespass of the hounds, could amount to intent to trespass.

Trespass by deposit of property on land

The LA succeeded in their claim of trespass against an election agent for fly posting political posters on various council properties and were able to recover the cost of removing the posters, *Hackney LBC v Arrowsmith* (2002). A right under a conveyance to enter land for the purposes of maintaining services did not extend to the installation of a new water pipe which was considered a new service, and the Court of Appeal held that the defendant was liable in trespass, *Martin v Childs* (2002).

Trespass by pollution transferred by watercourses

It would seem that a trespass claim can succeed if the person or object has been carried onto another's land by a current of water. A trespass claim succeeded in *Jones v Llanrwst UDC* (1911), when sewage was accidentally released into a river and caused pollution to the downstream riverbank. *Esso Petroleum v Southport Corporation* (1956), involved an unsuccessful claim in negligence in relation to pollution caused when a stranded oil tanker discharged oil in the sea in an attempt to lighten the vessel and refloat it. By *obiter*, the House of Lords stated that a claim in trespass would have failed as the pollution was not inevitable.

In *British Waterways Board v Severn Trent Water Ltd* (2001), a statutory sewerage undertaker (Severn Trent) discharging water into a canal without consent was considered trespass. ST's predecessor had a licence to discharge water into the canal for an annual fee, but BWB failed to negotiate an agreement with ST and cancelled the licence. The court of first instance held that ST had implied statutory authority to discharge surface water into a canal without consent. However the Court of Appeal, in allowing the appeal, stated that the judge had erred in her decision and ST did not have implied power and held that in the absence of an implied statutory authority, the discharge of water without consent amounted to trespass.

Trespass by airborne pollution

A claim from airborne pollution might not succeed in trespass, unless direct interference can be shown. In the case of spraying of pesticides or chemicals, it would have to be shown that the defendant sprayed directly over or onto the claimant's land, rather than the spray be carried by the air currents. In circumstances where direct interference can not be proved, then a claim in nuisance or *R. v F* could be considered instead. In *McDonald v Associated Fuels Ltd* (1954), a successful claim in negligence, the court stated trespass would also have succeeded on the facts. The defendant was blowing sawdust from his lorry into a storage bin. The exhaust fumes and sawdust were also blown into the plaintiff's home and the plaintiff was overcome by fumes and was injured. The defendant did not intend to cause the trespass, but he did intend to do the act which caused the trespass. The plaintiff succeeded in a claim for trespass in *Kerr v Revelstoke Building Materials Ltd* (1976), because the crop duster had flown directly over their farm.

The right to take action in trespass

The Court of Appeal held that a licensee, who did not own or occupy land, had sufficient interest in the land to be able to take out an injunction to stop the defendant from trespass on land and interfere with its plants, crops and land, *Monsanto Plc v Tilly* (2000). Monsanto was licensed to undertake trials of GM plants and crops at various locations. The defendants were anti–GM campaigners and had already uprooted some of Monsanto's crops. Monsanto took out injunctions to stop the defendants from trespass on land and interfering with its plants, crops and land at various trial sites. After the defendants were granted leave to appeal against the injunctions, Monsanto appealed to the Court of Appeal who held that the defendants could not rely on the defence of necessity or public interest in this particular case. Following the *Monsanto* case, in *Countryside Residential (NT) Ltd v Tugwell* (2000), the Court of Appeal held that developers who had a licence to carry out surveys in woods prior to obtaining planning permission, did not have sufficient interest in the land to obtain an order of possession against trespassers. Comparing to *Manchester Airport v Dutton* (1999), the judge stated there was a clear difference between a licence granted for the purpose of access, which did not provide effective control over the land, and a licence to occupy, which did. In this case, if the developers had already occupied the land, they may have been able to demonstrate sufficient interest.

Defences to trespass: Necessity, Licence to use the land
Remedies for trespass: Damages, injunction

PUBLIC NUISANCE (AS A TORT)

An individual can institute civil proceedings and claim damages in public nuisance, provided he can prove he has suffered 'particular' damage over and above that suffered by the rest of the class. It is not necessary to have an interest in land for a claim in public nuisance.

Civil Remedies for Public Nuisance: Damages, Injunction, Abatement.

THE FUTURE

The EU has prepared a draft directive for an Environmental Liability regime which will include damage to person and goods.

It may be that in the future, a person who has suffered loss or harm as a result of environmental pollution, will make a claim under this regime rather than tort.

---

5. THE PLANNING SYSTEM

The planning system, known as Development Control, controls land use and the development of the built environment and through this, plays a role in protecting the environment. Pollution from industries and other commercial activities is controlled and regulated by Environment Agency and local authorities (LAs) through IPC/PPC regulations. However, local planning authorities (LPAs) can also help regulate pollution or protect the environment through the planning system, either by refusing planning permission or by imposing conditions.

Development Control is based on laws that require planning permission from the LPA to change the current land use or build or alter existing property. The LPA can limit development or land use, by imposing conditions on the grant of planning permission. Development Plans are drawn up by LPAs, setting out policies for their area which take into account the requirements to provide a certain amount of new housing, together with economic, employment, social, political and environmental needs. Periodically, new development plans are prepared and adopted by the LPA. Planning permission is normally only granted if the application is in accordance with the local development plan policies. However, the LPA has the discretion to grant permission contrary to the plan if other material considerations indicate otherwise. Despite LPA's discretion, the system does provide some consistency in planning decisions and some certainty about the type of development allowed during the life of the development plan.

AGENCIES INVOLVED

The Planning Inspectorate Agency determines planning appeals, appeals against enforcement notices, inquiries for development plans and called-in planning applications. The Inspectorate has previously come under the Department of the

Environment, the DETR, DTLR, and since 2002 it has been an executive agency of the Office of the Deputy Prime Minister (ODPM). In Wales, the Planning Inspectorate reports to the National Assembly for Wales. References to the Secretary of State, refer to the Minister for the Government Department responsible for planning at the relevant time.

Local planning authorities (LPAs): Includes County, District, Unitary, Metropolitan Councils, National Parks and the Broads Authority.

Statutory Consultees who have to be consulted in the planning process and their views are taken into account. The appropriate statutory consultee(s) varies according to the category of development, and a full list is contained in Art.10, Town and Country Planning (General Development Procedure) Order 1995 (GDPO). Statutory consultees include: The Environment Agency, The Health and Safety Executive, The Secretary of State for Transport (now part of ODPM), The Secretary of State for Environment, Food and Rural Affairs or in Wales, the National Assembly of Wales, The Nature Conservancy Council for England (known as English Nature) or the Countryside Council for Wales in Wales, the waste regulation authority concerned and any LPAs likely to be affected by the development.

STATUTORY CONTROLS

The main planning Act is Town and Country Planning Act 1990 (TCPA 1990). There are a number of Town and Country Planning Regulations and Orders. Other Acts are Planning and Compensation Act 1991 (PACA 1991), Planning (Listed Building and Conversation Areas) 1990 and Planning (Hazardous Substances) Act 1990.

LOCAL PLANNING AUTHORITIES (LPAS)

- **County Councils:** responsible for structure plans. They can grant planning permission to themselves in certain circumstances and are consulted over some large-scale developments.
- **District Councils:** draw up local plans.
- **Unitary Authorities:** Since 1995, some District Councils have unitary status with responsibilities for all services.
- **National Parks:** make their own planning decisions and they are not determined by the local authority.

- **Norfolk and Suffolk Broads:** have their own planning authority.
- **Local parish, town councils:** Their views are considered in planning applications, but do not make planning decisions themselves.

DEVELOPMENT PLANS

Planning authorities have to produce outline development plans for their area, giving aims, policies, objectives and goals for their area. When a LPA considers planning applications, it refers to the policies of the development plan.

Types of development plans:

- **Structure Plans** are general strategic plans, by county council, National Park or unitary authority.
- **Local Plans** are more detailed plans, indicating specific land use policies, drawn up by district councils.
- **Unitary Development Plans** (UDP) replace Structure and Local Plans in London and metropolitan Areas, and a few non-metropolitan unitary authority areas. UDPs include the functions of both structure and local plans and incorporate minerals and waste policies.
- **Minerals and Waste local plans** are prepared by County and some unitary authorities and National Parks.

Government Guidance

The ODPM issue guidelines to LPAs. Regional Development Agencies prepare Regional Planning Guidance Notes which give the guidelines for both structure and local plans. Planning Policy Guidance Notes (PPGs) give guidelines on all aspects of planning, also Minerals Planning Guidance Notes. For the full list see the Planning Inspectorate website. Environmental considerations are required to be taken into account in preparing development plans, Town and Land Planning (Development Plan) Regulations (1999).

The structure plan is drawn up by a county or unitary planning authority taking into account the RPG for the region, PPGs and other relevant matters as listed in s.30(2). PPG 12 designates key land use issues: housing, including figures for new housing provision, green belts, the rural economy, the urban

economy, strategic transport and highway facilities and other
infrastructure needs, mineral works and protection of mineral
resources, waste treatment and disposal, land reclamation and
re-use, tourism, leisure and recreation and energy generation
including renewable energy. The Sec. Of State has the power to
call in the structure plan under s.35(a). Prior to adoption, invited
parties are allowed to make representations about the proposed
structure plan, and the planning inspector can make recommendations to the LPA.

Local plans have to conform with the general policies of the
structure plan. Any objectors, (*e.g.* land owners, local residents,
developers, local interest groups), should make their objections
known before the local plan is finalised, as all future planning
decisions will be based on planning policies set out in the local
plan. Once a draft plan has been has been prepared, it is available
for public inspection, s.40(2) and objectors have at least 6 weeks
to lodge objections. The plan may then be amended before a final
draft plan is placed 'on deposit' prior to being formally adopted.
A copy of the plan is sent to the Secretary of State who can require
the LPA to modify the plan, under s.43(4). Any unresolved
objections to the plan 'on deposit', necessitates a local inquiry
held by a planning inspector appointed by the Secretary of State.
Following the inquiry, the inspector makes recommendations
which the LPA does not have to accept, although it has to give
reasons for its decision. The Secretary of State has the power to
call the plan in and override the LPA's plan.

Challenges to development plans

Under s.287, a 'person aggrieved', has 6 weeks to challenge either
a structure plan modification or an adopted local plan in the high
court. Grounds of appeal being that the plan is *ultra vires* or there
has been a procedural error. Judicial review is another way in
which the adopted plan can be challenged.

In *Westminster CC v Great Portland Estates Plc* (1985), the House
of Lords held that *all* land use policies have to be included in the
plan. The court held that a LPA can withdraw a draft local plan or
proposals to alter or replace the existing local plan, at any time,
before it is adopted by the LA or approved by the Secretary of
State, *R. (Persimmon Homes) v North Hertfordshire DC* (2001).

In *Bovis Homes Ltd v New Forest DC* (2002), a building company
made a challenge under s.287 in relation to the adopted District
Local Plan. The Court held that the LPA erred in adopting the plan

on several counts, including apparent bias. However, the Court found the claimants rights under Art.6 of HRA 1998 were not breached as they could still make a planning application and under s.54a the LPA and have the power to grant permission contrary to the development plan. The Court dismissed a challenge to the structure plan by a developer under Art.6 HRA 1998, stating that if the civil rights of the claimant had been engaged, and he made no decision on the issue, the process meant those rights would not be breached, *JS Bloor v Swindon BC* (2001).

Material Consideration

Section 54a requires planning decisions to be made in accordance with local development plans unless material considerations indicate otherwise. In *St Albans DC v Secretary of State for the Environment* (1993), the court confirmed that under statute there was a presumption in favour of the development plan, but this could be rebutted if 'material considerations' indicate otherwise.

THE PLANNING PROCESS

The LPA regulate the development of land in its area through a system of 'development control', whereby 'planning permission' is required for any 'development', under s.57 of the TCPA 1990. 'Development' is defined under s.55(1), and includes: demolition of buildings, rebuilding, structural operations or additions to buildings, any operation normally undertaken by builders. Planning applications can be made for full, outline, retrospective or renewal of planning permission. Certain 3rd parties are informed of the application and given the right to represent their views. Anyone can make a representation, it is not necessary to have personal standing. Planning permission lapses if it is not acted upon within 5 years, and within 3 years for outline planning permission. Once planning permission has been given and acted upon it cannot be rescinded unless conditions have been placed on it. Certain developments which have greater impact on the environment require an EIA.

When determining an application, the LPA have to take into account the provisions of the development plan and any other material considerations, s.70(2). In *R. (Kides) v South Cambridgeshire DC* (2002), the Court of Appeal held that a LPA should have regard for any new 'material consideration' which arose after a resolution to grant permission but before the issue of the decision notice, but not necessary for the application to be referred back to the committee.

Change of Use

Planning permission is required for change of use of land, although Town and Country Planning (Use Classes) Order 1987 allows changes to similar land uses without the need for planning permission. A change of ownership of the land does not normally affect the right to continue to use the land for its existing use. A person wishing to ascertain that existing use of land is lawful and does not require planning permission, can apply to LPA who will issue a Certificate of lawfulness under s.191 and s.192 for proposed land use. Planning permission is not needed for an ancillary (secondary) use of the land, but it is required if it becomes the dominant use. The keeping of 44 dogs in a house was held to be a change of use, as it was considered that dog breeding had gone from ancillary to dominant use, *Wallington v Secretary of State for Wales* (1990). An intensification of use can also be a change of use, *Kensington & Chelsea RLBC v SSE* (1981). In *Thames Heliports Plc v Tower Hamlets LBC* (1997), the Court of Appeal held that use of navigable water can be considered a change of use.

Listed Buildings, Conservation Orders and Tree Preservation Orders

Planning (Listed Buildings and Conservation Areas) Act 1990 provides special planning policies for 'listed' buildings and buildings in Conservation Areas. All trees in Conservation Areas are automatically the subject of tree preservation orders, s.211. A LPA provides protection for trees by making Tree Preservation Orders under s.198, which prevents a tree from being cut or pruned without the LPA's consent.

Nature conservation and the planning system

Designated areas are afforded extra protection under planning law, these include: National Parks and Areas of Outstanding Natural Beauty (AONB), both designated by the Countryside Agency in England and the Countryside Council for Wales in Wales, Sites of Special Scientific Interest as designated by English Nature in England and Countryside Council for Wales in Wales, and the Broads. Stricter planning policies include the removal of permitted development rights under Art.1(5) of Town and Country Planning (GPD) Order 1995 to: National Parks, AONB, Conservation Areas, Areas specified by s.41(3) Wildlife and Countryside Act 1981, The Broads. Appropriate Bodies are consulted on planning applications as statutory consultees. EIAs are required in for 'sensitive areas' under The Town and Country Planning (EIA) (E &W) Regulations 1999.

Exemption for need for planning permission:

- **General Permitted Development Rights.** Town and Country Planning (General Permitted Development) Order 1995) (GPDO) grants automatic planning permission for certain classes of development, *e.g.* minor developments, developments carried out by a range of public services, including statutory undertakers.
- **Certain activities are not considered development**, such as the use of land for agriculture, even though they may have significant environmental impact.
- **Other activities are given automatic planning rights.** s.55 (2)(a)–(g) of the TCPA 1990 lists operations and uses of land that do not require planning permission, *e.g.* s.55(2)(f) permits the use of land for the purposes of agriculture or forestry (including afforestation) and the use for any of those purposes of any building occupied together with land so used.

If planning permission is not required, then there is no requirement for an EIA, even if the development is likely to have a significant impact on the environment. There are special rules for permitted development under Special Development Orders, Enterprise Zones and Simplified Planning Zones.

Conditions

LPA can make a condition attached to the grant of planning permission, s.70(1). In *Hall & Co Ltd v Shoreham on Sea UDC* (1964), the Court Of Appeal held that a condition attached to planning permission was unreasonable and therefore illegal. As the condition was void, the original planning permission itself was also void. House of Lords laid down guidelines for planning conditions in *Newbury DC v Secretary of State for the Environment*

(1981) that: a) They must be imposed for a planning purpose and not for an ulterior motive, b) they must reasonably and fairly relate to the development permitted; and c) they must not be perverse ('so unreasonable that no reasonable authority could have imposed them').

Section 106 Planning Obligations

The LPA may chose to enter into a s.106 'planning obligation' with the developer, which is easier to enforce than a condition. Section 106 agreements are made under deed and can only be made with a person who has a legal interest in the land and bind future owners and occupiers of the land. They can be drawn up and taken into account as a material consideration when the application is considered. A grant of planning permission will then be conditional on accepting the s.106 obligation. PACA 1991 revised s.106.

Planning conditions have to be enforced through enforcement notices, whereas s.106 agreements can be enforced by injunction, s.106(5). If the LPA fail to act, then affected 3rd parties, *i.e.* local residents, could consider civil action under Contracts (Rights of Third Parties) Act 1999. The Act only applies to contracts made after the Act came into force and applies to 3rd parties who are expressly identified in the contract by name, class or description but not necessary for the 3rd party to be in existence at the time the contract was made. A 3rd party can take action, a) where the contract expressly so provides, or b) where the contract confers a benefit to a 3rd party unless the contract indicates that the contracting parties did not intend the 3rd party to have rights of enforcement.

In *R. v Plymouth CC, Ex p. Plymouth and South Devon Co-op* (1993), the Court of Appeal dismissed Co-op's appeal and held that community benefits could be material considerations even when they were not to alleviate or overcome planning objections. The Court stated that 'Planning Obligation' had to satisfy the same tests as those laid out for conditions in Newbury DC case: a) it must have a planning purpose, b) it must fairly and reasonably relate to the permitted development, c) it must not be perverse or grossly unreasonable.

In *Tesco Stores Ltd v Secretary of State for the Environment* (1995), the House of Lords held that where a planning obligation offered by a developer under s.106 of TCPA 1990, related to a development, it was a material consideration within s.70(2) and regard should be made to it. The judge stated that planning obligation only had to satisfy a) and c) of the *Plymouth* case and that the connection only had to be more than *de minimis* connection with the proposed planning development. If an application was submitted with a s.106 obligation, then it was for the decision-maker to decide how much weight to attribute to it, and the court could not interfere unless the decision-maker had acted unreasonably as in the *Wednesbury* definition.

In 2003, proposals were announced by ODPM to allow developers to pay an optional charge instead of negotiating a s.106 agreement to fulfil their planning obligations.

Secretary of State's powers to determine planning application.

The Secretary of State has power to call in any planning application and take over jurisdiction from the LPA. This power is normally reserved for matters of national or regional importance. Recent inquiries include Finningley Airport, Dibden Terminal, Countryside and Rights of Way Act 2000, (Access Appeals), London Gateway (Shell Haven) and New Forest National Park .

Appeals against refusal of planning permission

If an applicant has been refused full planning permission, he can appeal and the case will be reviewed by a planning inspector on behalf of the Secretary of State. DETR Circular 05/2000 provides rules for the 3 planning appeal procedures, (written represen-tations, hearings and inquiries), for determining appeals under s.78.

Appeals against grant of planning permission

Under s.284 and s.288, an 'Aggrieved person' is able to apply to High Court to challenge a decision on 'a question of law'. The LPA is also able to apply to the High Court to challenge a decision made by a planning inspector. The High Court is not able to make planning decisions, but will refer the case back to be redetermined. Decisions by the LPA can also be challenged by judicial review, but decisions by the Secretary of State can only be challenged under s.288. Third parties do not have a right of appeal against the grant of planning permission.

JUDICIAL REVIEW

A judicial review can also be used to challenge the decision of the LPA if it did not take all material considerations into account or that the decision-making process were flawed in another way. Apart from the planning applicant, any interested party can take a judicial review, provided 'standing' can be shown. When assessing whether a challenge is within the time limit, in *R. (Burkett) v Hammersmith & Fulham LBC* (2002), the House of Lords held that grounds for an application for judicial review arose from the actual grant of planning permission.

HUMAN RIGHTS AND HUMAN RIGHTS ACT 1998 (HRA 1998)

Since the European Convention of Human Rights has been incorporated into UK law through the HRA 1998, there have been a number of challenges to planning decisions on human rights grounds. In particular Art.8(1), Art.1 of the 1st protocol and Art.6(1). Under the planning system, 3rd parties do not have any rights of appeal against the grant of planning permission, issue of a certificate of lawfulness, the LPA or Secretary of State's decision that an EIA is not required or refusal of the LPA to take enforcement action. As a consequence, a number of cases have recently considered whether the current planning system complies with Art.6, *'right to a fair and public hearing by an independent and impartial tribunal'*.

In *Bryan v UK* (ECHR) (1995), Bryan had unsuccessfully appealed to a planning inspector and High Court, on points of law, to overturn an enforcement notice and finally applied to ECHR. The ECHR dismissed the case, as Art.6 requirements had been satisfied by the High Court's review, which had considered whether the inspector's decision had been made in accordance with principles of openness, fairness and impartiality. In a group of cases, known as the *Alconbury* Case (2001), the House of Lords had to consider if the Secretary of State's dual role in formulating policy and decisions on applications, meant that the process was impartial and independent. Allowing the appeal by the Secretary of State, the House of Lords stated that his powers to determine planning applications were not incompatible with Art.6(1) of the HRA 1998. The reason being that the courts were able to exercise sufficient control, through judicial review, over the decision-making part of the Secretary of State's role. The Court did not

have to exercise control over the policy-making part of the
Secretary of State's role, as in *Bryan v UK* (ECHR) (1995).

The High Court dismissed claims by residents that their rights
to 'fair and public' hearing under Art.6 of HRA 1998 had been
breached as there had not been a public inquiry, *R. (Vetterlein) v
Hampshire CC* (2001). The Judge stated that as the other grounds
had failed, the issue regarding a public hearing did not arise, and
even if it did, the procedure implemented by the LPA gave them
such an opportunity. In *BT Plc v Gloucester CC* (2001), where
the grant of planning permission lead to an application for
Compulsory Purchase Order for BT's land, the High Court found
the availability of judicial review avoided an infringement of BT's
rights to a fair trial under Art.6.

R. (Friends Provident Life) v Secretary of State for TLR (2001),
involved an application for a retail development to be partly
owned by the LA itself. The Court dismissed a judicial review by
FP, owners of a nearby development, who had argued that their
rights under Art.6 had been breached as the Secretary of State had
failed to call the application in. *R. (Cummin) v Camden LBC, the
Secretary of State for ETR* (2001) concerned the grant of planning
permission by the Council for 3 applications from its own Leisure
Services Department on its own land. The judge stated that the
Council had not acted in a way which was incompatible with
Art.6 because of the courts jurisdiction and by way of a judicial
review nor had the Secretary of State acted incompatibly with his
obligations under Art.6.

The Court rejected claims of a breach of claimants rights to a
determination by an independent and impartial tribunal under
Art.6, in *R. (Kathro) v Rhondda Cynon Taff CBC* (2001). However,
the Judge stated that, '*in my view a real possibility that, in certain
circumstances involving disputed issues of fact, a decision of a LPA
which is not itself an independent and impartial tribunal might not be
subject to sufficient control by the court to ensure compliance with Art.6
overall.*' In *R. (Adlard) v Secretary of State for ETR* (2002), the Court
of Appeal dismissed the applicants claim that their rights under
Art.6 had been breached as the Secretary of State did not to call in
a planning application, thus denying them an oral hearing for
their objections, The Court held: 1) when considering whether
Art.6 was satisfied it also had to take into account the High
Court's review jurisdiction. If, in a particular case, the LPA had
acted unfairly or unreasonably in denying an objector any or
sufficient oral hearing, then the court would quash the decision.
2) The Secretary of State was only obliged to ensure his actions

were not incompatible with Convention rights and not the actions of others.

SCIENTIFIC UNCERTAINTY, HEALTH RISKS AND THE PLANNING SYSTEM

The public have concerns over pollution emitting industries being sited in close proximity to residential areas because of the possible risks to human health. There are also health fears regarding electromagnetic radiation (EMFs) from power lines and telecommunications transmitters, including mobile phone masts and TETRA police radio masts. Under EU law, there is a policy of the precautionary principle under Art.174 (ex 130r) EC Treaty. In the *R. v Secretary of State for Trade and Industry Ex p. Duddridge* (1995), the Court of Appeal held that the Secretary of State was not obliged to adopt the precautionary principle for national policies unless required to do so by an EU Directive. The Court of Appeal held that public concern about safety is a material consideration for a planning application, even if the public perception of danger was unfounded, *Newport CBC v Secretary of State for Wales and Browning* (1997).

A Grant of planning permission can be challenged under judicial review if the decision makers did not take into account material considerations of health risks, or perceived health risks to the residents or their human rights under the Human Rights Act 1998. The Courts only have the power to quash permission and order the LPA/inspector to redetermine the case. The decision makers have to take into account factors they previously omitted, but it is up to them to decide how much weight to give to such factors and they may come to the same decision as before.

Power lines and health risk

The *Duddridge* Case related to power lines being laid under a residential area and the residents concerns about the possible health risk. Electricity power lines do not require planning permission as they have the benefit of permitted development rights. However, permission is needed to install electricity lines under, on or over private land. The Electricity Company can come to a voluntary agreement with the landowner and/or occupier, but if unable to do so, they can apply to the Department of Trade and Industry for a necessary electricity wayleave, under s.10 of the Electricity Act 1989. Some LPAs have tried unsuccessfully to incorporate a policy of 'prudent avoidance' in relation to building near to power lines. The inspector's report for Hambleton District local plan in 1997 stated, *'new development should be sited well away from power lines ... a "prudent precaution" on public health grounds'*, but recommended against adopting a specific policy. Lincoln DC's 1997 draft local plan suggested a corridor of land within 50 metres of high voltage cable which would not be used for development of new housing, education and employment uses. The Inspector's report recommended this policy be removed, stating such policy issues should be resolved at a national level.

Telecommunications transmitters and health risk

Telecommunications transmitters, including mobile phone masts and TETRA masts, under certain height limits also enjoy permitted developments rights under the General Permitted Development Order 1995, as amended by 1999 and 2001 Orders. When planning permission is not required, the operator still requires 'prior approval' from the LPA. The Stewart Inquiry into 'Telecommunications Mast Development' published its report in 2000. It recommended a precautionary approach to mobile phone masts and permitted development rights for all base stations be revoked and new base stations be subject to the normal planning process. Following the report, PPG 8 for Telecommunications was revised in 2001. Paragraph 29 states that health considerations and public concern can be material considerations in determining applications for planning permission and prior approval, however, para.31 states that it does not provide for a precautionary approach.

Once a mast has been erected, any local residents who have been adversely affected by the siting of the mast, can lodge an objection with the operator. They have 3 months in which to make an objection to the mast under s.10 of the Telecommunication Act 1984 (para.17 of Sch.2), which provides for objection to overhead apparatus. If the operator does not resolve the matter to the satisfaction of the objector, he can apply to the County Court for the objection to be upheld.

In *R. v Tanbridge DC Ex p. Al Fayed* (2000), the Court of Appeal allowed a judicial review to be heard regarding planning permission for a telephone mast on the grounds that the possible health risks had not been properly considered. However, it rejected the challenge, as even if the correct procedure had been followed, the HSE would have reached the same conclusion.

In *R. (Herman) v Winchester CC* (2001), the Court quashed planning permission for a mobile phone mast near a school and ordered the application to be redetermined. On redetermination by the LPA, planning permission was refused, the operator appealed and after a local inquiry, was granted permission in 2003. The court gave leave for a judicial review in *R. (Smith) v Stockport MBC* (2001), on the grounds that the LPA did not consider the perceived health risk. The case did not proceed to a full hearing as the mobile phone operator gave a commitment to the court that it would not erect a mast after all. The high court dismissed a challenge to the grant of planning permission for 3 communications masts in Stroud on the grounds that the planning inspector had taken into account the public's perceived health fears, but on the facts, they did not justify refusing permission, *Trevett v Secretary of State for TLR* (2002).

R. (Philips) v First Secretary of State, Havant BC, Hutchison 3G (UK) Ltd (2003), concerned a challenge, over the grant of planning permission for a mobile phone mast, by a concerned local resident. The challenge was made under s.288 of the Town and Country Planning Act 1990 and was allowed by the Judge on the grounds of procedural unfairness as the mast company had not considered other alternative sites as required by PPG 8.

Perceived health risk and Art.8 of the Human Rights Act 1998

The Court dismissed a challenge by local residents who claimed that given the link between the quality of life and pollution, the grant of planning permission for an incinerator near their home, breached their rights under Art.8, *R. (Vetterlein) v Hampshire CC* (2001).

ENFORCEMENT OF PLANNING REGULATIONS

The LPA can take enforcement action against a person who fails to comply with notice served by the LPA for unauthorised development.

1) **Planning contravention notices.** Where the LPA thinks there may be a breach of planning control, it may serve notices on any owner, occupier or other person who is using or carrying out operations on land, seeking to find out information about land use or occupation, s.171(c). It

is a summary offence to ignore a planning contravention notice, or knowingly provide incorrect information, s.171(d).

2) **Breach of condition notices.** The LPA can serve a written notice on the person responsible for non-compliance of condition, requiring compliance within a period of not less than 28 days, s.187(a). Non-compliance leads to a fine and further fines for continuing non-compliance.

3) **Enforcement notices** Section 172 allows enforcement notice to be served on a LPA in respect of unauthorised development. Notices must be served on all owners and occupiers of relevant premises, including licensees. The enforcement notice must specify the alleged breach, the steps required to remedy the breach, the reason the notice is issued and the relevant land. The notice gives the time within which it has to be complied with, a minimum of 28 days. At the end of this period, if the owner (or the person in control of or person with interest in the land) has not complied, it becomes a criminal offence, s.179. Compliance with an enforcement notice does not discharge it, as under s.181 the notice attaches permanently to the land.

4) **Stop notices** If, having served an enforcement notice, the LPA require someone to stop carrying out unlawful activity, then it may serve a stop notice under s.183 of the TPCA 1990. If the person fails to stop the activity, they will be given same penalty as breach of enforcement activity. The person can apply for retrospective planning permission.

The maximum penalty for these offences on summary conviction, is £20,000 in the magistrates court to unlimited fine on indictment (in the crown court). The magistrates court can send a case to the crown court for sentencing. Under s.178, the LA has the power to enter the land and remedy the breach at the owner's expense. Section 188 requires LPAs to keep public register of enforcement notices, stop notices and breach of condition notices.

Injunctions can also be taken against actual or anticipated breaches of planning permission under PACA 1991.

ENFORCEMENT ACTION AND HUMAN RIGHTS

The ECHR rejected claims by 5 British Gypsy families, in *Chapman v UK (ECHR)* (2001), that lack of access to a court to appeal against planning decision and an enforcement notice breached Art.6, that the enforcement measures would deprive their children of an education under Art.2 of 1st protocol or interfere with their peaceful enjoyment of their land under Art.1 of 1st Protocol or that there had been a breach of Art.14 which prohibits discrimination. Another case heard by ECHR, concerned a gipsy woman who had sited caravans on her land, to be near family members, without planning permission. The LPA issued an enforcement notice and fined her for failing to comply with notice. At an interim hearing, the ECHR found her rights had been violated under Art.8, but at the final hearing, found against her, *Buckley v UK* (ECHR)(1996).

4 cases brought by gypsy families in the English courts, in *South Bucks DC v Porter* (2001), concerned whether injunctions brought under s.178 to restrain a breach of planning control, breached their rights under Art.8(1) of HRA 1998 and if such measures were proportionate. The Court of Appeal held that it had a duty to act proportionately, weighing the need to fulfil the public interest criteria but that the private interests of an individual should not be excessively burdened. It allowed 3 of the appeals, having taken into account the relevant circumstances of each family, the hardship caused by the need to move, availability of alternative sites, consequences to family health and education, extent of alleged breach of planning control and prior planning decisions.

In *Salisbury DC v Le Roi* (2001) the Court of Appeal stated that it was possible for a claim under Art.8 to defeat a planning enforcement action, but not in this case. The appellant was not occupying the premises and had denied any intention of residing there, so demolishing the barn would not deprive him and his family of accommodation. The Court of Appeal allowed an appeal for a judicial review of an enforcement and stop notice, under s.178, on the grounds that the demolition of the building would deprive the applicant of the property or interfere with her peaceful enjoyment, in breach of Art.1. The Court held that there was merit in the application, and the LPA would have to review its decision now that the Convention had been incorporated into English Law, *R. (Hadfield) v Macclesfield BC* (2001).

In a case involving an appeal against an enforcement notice, *New Forest DC v Duffy* (2001), a Planning Inspector agreed that to demolish property not complying with a condition of planning permission (agricultural occupancy), would infringe the rights of the family under HRA 1998. On appeal to the High Court by the

LPA, the case was referred back to be redetermined. After a local inquiry, the Secretary of State made the determination in 2003. He agreed with the 2nd Inspector that to uphold the enforcement notice and demolish the property would be a disproportionate infringement of the family rights under Art.8. The Secretary of State also agreed that the HRA 1998 does not extend to protect against having to move to a less commodious house. The enforcement notice was quashed and planning permission was granted for 3 years with certain conditions.

Planning permission and nuisance

A grant of planning permission does not give immunity from causing a nuisance, *e.g.* (private) nuisance or statutory nuisance.

FUTURE LEGISLATION

The Government published proposals for reform of the planning system in a Green Paper, 'Planning: Delivering a Fundamental Change' in 2001, followed in 2002 by Policy Statement, 'Sustainable Communities: Delivering through Planning'. National Assembly for Wales published its own consultation paper: 'Planning: Delivering for Wales' in 2002, which was followed by its planning policy. As a result of these policy statements, the Planning and Compulsory Purchase Bill, has been introduced in the 2002–2003 Parliamentary session. The Bill's proposals include replacing RPG with Regional Spatial Strategies (RSS), which will set out Government policies in relation to land use and development under the auspices of the proposed Regional Assemblies. County Structure Plans will be abolished, although County Councils will retain responsibility for waste and mineral plans. Local development frameworks will replace local plans and the life of planning permission will be reduced from 5 years to 3 years. Concerns have been voiced by environmental campaign groups that the loss of structure plans will reduce the opportunity for community participation at county level, together with very limited provision for participation in the preparation of a Regional Spatial Strategy. The proposed bill does not provide for any 3rd party rights of appeal, although the Scottish Executive has announced that it intends to have a consultation into the issues and options for 3rd party appeals in planning during 2003.

In 2003, the ODPM issued a consultation on a draft Planning Policy Statement (PPS) on Renewable Energy which will replace PPG 22. The PPS 22 will cover onshore wind generation from turbines, but not offshore wind turbines, as they are not subject to the land use planning system. In 2003, The Scottish Parliament debated the growing concerns over proliferation of planning applications for onshore wind farms throughout Scotland, with some SMPs asking for a moratorium on planning decisions until new planning guidance could be drawn up.

The Government has drawn up draft guidance on environmental assessments required under 2001 EU Strategic Environmental Assessment Directive on the assessment of the effects of certain plans and programmes on the environment.

6. ENVIRONMENTAL IMPACT ASSESSMENT (EIA)

EIAs originated in the early 1970's in the US. In the UK, they have been introduced into the planning process through EU directives and certain developments now have to be accompanied by an EIA. LPAs have always been able to consider the effects of a proposed development on the environment when taking all material considerations into account, an EIA allows a more uniform and formal approach.

EIA INTRODUCED THROUGH EU DIRECTIVES

EIAs were introduced into UK law following the 1985 Directive on the Assessment of the Effects of Certain Private and Public Projects on the Environment and later amended by 1997 Directive on Environmental Impact (amendment).

UK Law

The 1985 Directive was implemented into domestic law through Town and Country Planning (Assessment of Environmental Effects) Regulations 1988. Section 71a was added to the TCPA

1990, giving the Secretary of State powers to extend the categories of projects (or developments) requiring an environmental assessment. The Secretary of State used these powers to introduce Town and Country Planning (Assessment of Environmental Effects (Amendment) Regulations 1994 which extends the classes of project to be subject to an environmental assessment, *e.g.* wind turbines, motorway service stations.

The 1997 Directive was transposed into UK law through Town and Country Planning (EIA) Regulations 1999 (1999 Regulations). Following the 1999 Regulations, the 'Environmental Assessment' became known as the 'Environmental Impact Assessment'. The Government is able to bring in new regulations to amend the current regulation or Act through Statutory Instruments. The Government issued guidelines on EIA through DETR Circular 02/99, 'Environment Impact Assessment'.

There are two aspects to EIA:
  1) the process
  2) the issues it raises for the courts: a) whether a planning application should have had an EIA or b) has the EU Directive(s) been adequately transposed in domestic law.

EU DIRECTIVE ADEQUATELY TRANSPOSED INTO DOMESTIC LAW

The court held that the 1985 Directive had a direct effect in *Twyford Parish Council v Secretary of State for Environment* (1993). The requirement to carry out an Environmental Assessment was directly effective in relation to those projects listed in Annex 1 of the Directive where an environmental assessment was mandatory.

In *R. v North Yorkshire CC Ex p. Brown* (1998), the House of Lords held that an application to reactivate mineral extraction under Planning And Compensation Act 1991(PACA 1991) did require an EIA before the LPA imposed new conditions. The LPA unsuccessfully argued that an EIA was only required under the Directive when the original development consent was granted. In *R. v Durham CC, Sherburn Stone Co. and the Secretaray of State for ETR Ex p. Huddleston* (2000), a local resident successfully challenged that the deemed grant of planning permission was contrary to the 1985 Directive, which required EIAs in respect of proposed mineral extraction operations. The Court of Appeal held that the EU Directive was directly effective where it had been ineffectively transposed in UK law and the statutory default provision, in Sch.2 of PACA 1991, was ineffective. The Court of Appeal held that in relation to urban development projects, the 1999 Regulation had properly transposed the 1997 EU Directive, *Berkeley v Secretary of State for ETR (No.3)* (2001).

WHAT IS EIA?

EIA is the process of gathering the information, which is carried out by the developer and other bodies, so the LPA can determine the environmental effects of the development before making the planning decision. It is similar to having to take all material considerations into account. The report produced from the information is called the environmental statement. LPA will make an assessment based on the information collected by:

- The applicant giving details of the impact on the environment and any plans to reduce the effects.
- Statutory undertakers (*e.g.* Environment Agency, English Nature).
- Other independent 3rd parties (*e.g.* local conservation groups).
- Members of the public.
- Planning authority itself.

Where an application is accompanied by an EIA, Reg.3 prohibits a grant of planning permission unless the environmental information has been taken into account by the decision makers and their decision states they have done so. Under Reg.19, a LPA can ask for further information following the EIA. The LPA is able to grant planning permission even if the development has negative environmental impact and does not have to impose conditions to reduce any negative environmental impact. To discharge their legal obligations, the decision-makers only have to take all material considerations into account when making their decision, otherwise their decision can be challenged by a judicial review.

Environmental Statement

The EIA contains an Environmental Statement. This statement has to contain certain information as required by Sch.4, including:

- Description of project including size, description and design.
- main effects the development likely to have on environment (type and quantities of expected residues and emissions (water, air and soil pollution, noise, vibration, light, heat, radiation, etc.).
- measure to be taken to avoid or reduce any significant adverse effects.
- alternatives studied by applicant or appellant & reason for choice.
- Aspects of environment likely to be affected by development.
- Non–technical Summary.

PROJECTS WHICH REQUIRE AN EIA

Sch.1 developments

An EIA is mandatory for all developments listed under Sch.1 of 1999 Regulations: *e.g.* crude oil refineries, larger thermal power stations, motorways, major roads, chemical installations, pig & poultry units, groundwater abstractions. Modifications to Sch.1 projects also come under Sch.1. Where there is uncertainty, the Secretary of State or the LPA can make a ruling as to whether a project falls under Sch.1.

Sch.2 developments may require an EIA

Sch.2 developments (including thermal power stations (under certain heat output), golf courses over one hectare, motorway service stations, urban developments (*e.g.* multiplex cinema)) require an EIA to be carried out if the project will have a significant effect on the environment. The Court quashed outline planning permission in *BT Plc v Gloucester CC* (2001), stating that the LPA had applied the wrong test as it had considered the assessment to be necessary only where there were significant adverse effects, it should have also considered significant beneficial effects.

Sch.3 has the selection criteria for screening Sch.2 developments. Some proposed Sch.2 developments have a threshold criteria, for guidance, but these thresholds are removed for 'sensitive' areas. Sensitive areas are listed in Reg.2(1) and include Sites of Special Scientific Interest, European site under

Conservation (Natural Habitats.) Regulations 1994, National Parks, World Heritage Sites and AONB. Under Reg.4(8) the Secretary of State has powers to request an EIA, and under Reg.4(4) can direct that a development is exempt. In *R. (Malster) v Ipswich BC* (2001), the Court held that the 1999 Regulations were not concerned with individual properties and whilst the development might have a significant impact on a few properties this did not necessarily mean there would be a significant impact on the environment.

The extent of LPA's discretion over EIA

LPAs have some discretion in deciding whether a Sch.2 development will have a significant effect on the environment and therefore whether it will require an EIA. Prior to Court of Appeal case, *R. (Goodman) v Lewisham BC* (2003), it had only been possible to challenge a LPA's determination that an EIA was not required on the grounds of wednesbury unreasonableness. In *R. v Swale BC Ex p. RSPB* (1991), the Court held that it was for the LPA to decide whether a project fell between Sch.1 or Sch.2 and this judgment was followed in *R. v Wirral MBC Ex p. Gray* (1997). However, in *R. (Goodman) v Lewisham LBC* (2003) the Court of Appeal quashed a grant of outline planning permission, on the grounds that the LPA's decision that the development did not fall within a Sch.2 category was wrong in law. The case concerned whether a proposed development was an 'infrastructure project' and an 'urban development project' and the court held that if the LPA's understanding of those expressions was wrong in law then the court must correct the error and Wednesbury reasonableness could not be applied to the determination of statutory expressions.

Decision maker can not dismiss the requirement for EIA

It is no longer sufficient for a LPA to argue that it has all the information required and a formal EIA would not provide any additional information. An LPA granted itself planning permission without considering whether an EIA was required in *R. v Poole BC Ex p. BeeBee* (1991). The judge held that the LPA had all the relevant information and environmental statement would have been superfluous (this case would be decided differently now). In *Berkeley v Secretary of State for the Environment* (2000), the House of Lords quashed planning permission for redevelopment of Fulham Football Club under s.288 of the TCPA 1990, on the grounds that it was *ultra vires*, having been made without the consideration as to the need for an EIA. The House of Lords overturned the decision of Court of Appeal, stating that where planning permission had been granted in respect of a project likely to have a significant effect on the environment, a court was not entitled retrospectively to dispense with the requirement of an EIA on the grounds that the outcome would have been the same or that the LPA or Secretary of State had all the information necessary to enable them to reach a proper decision on the environmental issues. In *Bellway URS v Gillespie* (2003), a proposed housing development was to be built on an old gas works site and residents successfully challenged the Secretary of State's decision that an EIA was not needed. The Court of Appeal held that mitigating measures should be considered as part of the EIA process and the decision maker could not dispense with the need for an EIA on the grounds that conditions can be imposed on the grant of planning permission which will prevent significant environmental effects.

Permitted Developments subject to EIA criteria

Permitted Developments did fall outside the scope of EIA, but are now included when the proposed development meets the criteria of Sch.1 or Sch.2. If a LPA determines a proposed development under permitted development rights does not come under Schs1 or 2, it will not require an EIA. *R. v Wirral MBC Ex p. Gray* (1997), concerned an extension of a chemical plant which the LPA considered did not require an EIA under Sch.2. The court held that as the proposed development did not require an EIA, it was able to proceed under permitted development rights.

Projects not requiring planning permission

Certain projects that do not require planning permission continue to be dealt with separately under specific regulations.

Transboundary implications

Consultation is required between member states where any development is likely to have significant environmental effects on another member state.

Incremental development may need EIA

If a developer applies for the land to be developed in stages, the LPA should consider the whole development rather than just the application before them.) In *R. v Swale BC Ex p. RSPB* (1991), a planning application for Lappel Bank did not include an EIA and RSPB challenged on the grounds that it was part of a larger development. The application failed, but the Court stated that the LPA should look beyond what was applied for, to see if the application was part of a more substantial development.

Outline Planning Permission and EIA

Outline planning permission can be granted for a development which requires an EIA provided the permission is restricted so that development which can take place is within the boundaries of matters assessed in the environmental statement. The High Court quashed a grant of outline planning permission for a large business park, to be developed in the next 10–15 years in *R. v Rochdale MBC Ex p. Tew* (2000). The Court held it was not possible for full environmental information to be available for public scrutiny as the full size and scale of the development could not be provided. However, the Court of Appeal dismissed a challenge in *R. v Rochdale MBC Ex p. Milne* (2002), where the same LPA had attached conditions relating to the EIA with the grant the outline planning permission. In *R. (Barker) v Bromley LBC* (2001), the Court of Appeal stated that the LPA did not have to assess the need for an EIA at both the time outline planning permission was granted and at the time reserved matters were considered. Following a further appeal by the applicant, the House of Lords has referred the matter to the ECJ for a preliminary ruling under Art.234.

SCREENING

Before submitting a planning application, a developer can ask the LPA for an opinion as to whether an EIA is required and The LPA has to issue an opinion within 3 weeks. If a planning application is submitted without an environment statement and the LPA has not already been issued a screening opinion, it has to decide whether the development falls within the category that requires an EIA. In *Fernback v Harrow LBC* (2000), the court held that after giving a negative screening opinion, the LPA may subsequently

determine that the development requires an EIA. A decision that
an EIA was not required was quashed in *R. v St Edmundsbury BC
Ex p. Walton* (1999) as the decision had been made by a officer
without formal delegated powers.

Following 1999 Regulations, Reg.21 requires the decision
maker to give reasons for the grant of refusal of any planning
applications accompanied by an EIA, whereas previously only
required when planning permission refused. However, while
Reg.4(6) imposes a duty to give reasons why a proposed
development is an EIA development, the decision maker does not
have to give reasons why an EIA is not required. In *R. v Secretary
of State for ETR and Parcelforce Ex p. Marson* (1998), a proposed
development for a sorting facility came within Sch.2, but the
Secretary of State did not think it would have a significant
environmental effect and no further reasons were given. The
Court of Appeal held there was nothing in National law or EU
law that required more information to be given.

SCOPING

Under Reg.10 of the 1999 Regulations, developers are now able to
ask the LPA, before an application is submitted, what issues it
wants to be addressed in an environmental statement. If
necessary, further information can be requested after the EIA has
been considered by the LPA. In *R. v Cornwall Ex p. Hardy* (2001),
the LPA were advised by English Nature that bats might be
present on the site although the applicant had not addressed this
issue. The LPA attached a condition of planning permission that
the developer carry out a survey to establish whether bats were
present prior to starting the development. The Court quashed the
grant of planning permission as all the relevant information had
not been provided in the environmental statement.

EFFECTIVE OF THE SYSTEM

The fact that an application requires an EIA does not necessarily
mean that the application will be refused. However, it encourages
the developer to consider the measures to mitigate any damage to
the environment or alternative at an early stage of the proposal.
The system does not provide for 3rd party rights of appeal
against a determination that an EIA is not required. Should a

proposed development be exempt from planning permission and it is not covered by other specific EIA regulations, then it avoids the scrutiny of an EIA even though the development may have a significant effect on the environment. There is no requirement for post-project monitoring of developments requiring EIA.

FUTURE LEGISLATION

The 2001 EU Directive on the assessment of the effects of certain plans and programmes on the environment (SEA Directive) is due to be implemented by member states in 2004. The Directive requires an environmental assessment to be undertaken by the statutory bodies when preparing certain plans. It will be applied in the preparation of Regional Planning Guidance and Local Authority Development Plans under the present planning system and the proposed Regional Spatial Strategies and Local Development Frameworks.

7. EU AND INTERNATIONAL ENVIRONMENTAL LAW

INTERNATIONAL ENVIRONMENTAL LAW

International law is only briefly discussed here, to illustrate its role within domestic environmental legislation. International law does not have a direct effect on national law, until states (countries) introduce domestic legislation after voluntarily ratifying an international treaty. An international treaty is the end result of the international community meeting up at a conference (also called a convention) to consider particular global or international environmental concerns.

Some treaties deal with concerns regarding 'global commons', that is natural resources beyond the territories of individual countries, *e.g.* international waters. Others might deal with activities by countries which have a more localised impact, but nevertheless still adversely affect neighbouring countries, *e.g.* air pollution or pollution of an international river. At a convention, if delegates can establish common strategies to tackle concerns(s), they can then be put forward into a treaty (also called a convention or an agreement). These strategies might consist of 'soft law' which can be declarations, recommendations or principles, or 'hard law', consisting of specific standards which are then incorporated into domestic legislation.

It may take several years for the treaty to be drafted to the satisfaction of all participating states. A treaty is authenticated when the state representatives sign the treaty, but a state does not become legally bound by the treaty until it ratifies it. A state ratifies a treaty when it is ready to adopt the terms of the treaty into its domestic legislation. A treaty will specify how many states must ratify, before it enters into force. Although a state may send their ministers to an international convention and become a signatory to the treaty, it may not be in a position to ratify for some years. A 'protocol' is a sub-agreement to a treaty. Under the terms of a treaty, the parties agree to meet at regular intervals to review progress and consider new developments.

The major international treaties are organised by the United Nations or other UN bodies such as UNEP. The first international conference to consider environment needs was the UN conference on the Human Environment (Stockholm, 1972). The conference led to the setting up of the UN Environment Program (UNEP) and the Stockholm Declaration and Action Plan. The conference defined principles for the preservation and enhancement of the natural environment and highlighted some of problems of industrialised countries, such as acid rain and habitat degradation. The UN set up the World Commission on Environment and Development (UNCED, also known as the Bruntland Commission) in the 1980's. In 1987, UNCED produced the Bruntland Report on 'Our Common Future', which gave the structure to Agenda 21 and the principles of the 1992 Rio Declaration. It also gave the definition of sustainable development, *'development that meets the needs of the present without comprising the ability of future generations to meet their own needs'*.

The 1992 UNCED Rio Conference (the Earth Summit), produced a number of legal texts, including:

a) **Rio Declaration:** on the Environment and Development, which produced a number of 'soft law' principles. Principle 1 states that *'human beings are at the centre of concerns for sustainable development They are entitled to a* *healthy and productive life in harmony with nature'*. Principle 15 refers to the precautionary principle, Principle 10 provides for the public awareness and participation in environmental decision making, Principle 16 refers to polluter pays principle, Principle 17 refers to the need for environmental impact assessments.

b) **UN Framework Convention on Climate Change,** which subsequently produced the 1997 Kyoto Protocol on Global Warming.

c) **Convention on Biological Diversity**

d) **Agenda 21:** A global action plan, which has been incorporated into EU and UK law.

The UK is a party to a number of major international environmental treaties. Treaty secretariats normally maintain a website giving all relevant information about the treaty, including current ratification status.

THE EUROPEAN UNION

EU Environment Law

EU environmental policies have had a huge impact on UK, with over 80 per cent of UK environmental law legislation being derived from the European Union. The EU has produced over 200 legal texts on environmental measures, most of which have been in the form of directives which have then been transposed into UK law. Over 40 per cent of EU enforcement action is in relation to environmental laws. EU Environmental law has to be based on one or more provisions of the EC Treaty. The Original Treaty of Rome, did not contain any environmental legislation. Following the 1972 UN Stockholm Convention, the EEC adopted its first environmental polices with an Action Programme (see more about Action Programmes below) which were then developed into community law. However, there was no specific legislation to provide for environmental policies until the Single European Act (SEA) 1986. Until then, environmental legislation was enacted on the basis of harmonisation laws under Art.94 (ex 100) and the EC's general powers under Art.308 (ex 235). The Environment was formally adopted into EU policy through the Single European Act 1986, when Arts174–176 (ex 130r–t) was incorporated into the Treaty of Rome. The Treaty on European Union 1992 (TEU, also known as Maastricht Treaty), amended

Art.2 of the EC Treaty of Rome to provide for sustainable growth in respect of the environment and Art.3 introduce a general environmental sphere to policy.

PROVISIONS FOR EU ENVIRONMENTAL LAW UNDER ARTS 174–6

- Art.174 (ex130r) sets out environmental policy: *Preserving, protecting and improving the quality of the environment, Protecting human health, Prudent and rational utilisation of natural resources, Promoting measures at international level to deal with regional or worldwide environmental problems.*
- Art.175 (ex 130s) provides the authority for environmental legislation the environmental action programmes.
- Art.176 provides for member states to introduce more stringent measures to protect the environment provided they are compatible with the Treaty.

How Environmental legislation is adopted

Environmental legislation can be enacted under:

- **Art.95 (harmonising of the single market).** In SEA 1996, Art.95 was amended so that when considering measures in relation to environmental protection, it would take a high level of protection as its base. This illustrated that environmental measures could be considered under harmonising legislation, not just Art.175. The Maastricht Treaty introduced the co-decision procedure to Art.95, giving the European Parliament a greater involvement in formulating legislation.
- **Art.175 (environmental measures).** Art.175 was introduced by SEA 1986. The co-decision procedure was introduced for Art.175 by Amsterdam Treaty.

Where environmental measures could be taken under either Arts 95 or 175, there has been some dispute, particularly when they had different adopting procedures. In *Commission v Council (1991) (Titanium Dioxide Case)*, originally legislation had been put forward under Art.95, then the Council decided to adopt it under Art.175. The ECJ found that the legislation for environmental and harmonisation legislation should use Art.95. However, in *Commission v Council (Waste Disposal) (1993)*, the EJC reversed the decision.

In 2003 the Council adopted a Framework Decision on protecting the environment through criminal law under Art.34(2)(b)TEU (Maastricht Treaty). Alternative legislation being considered was a Framework Directive under Art.175 EC Treaty, which failed to be adopted. The European Commission, supported by the European Parliament, has applied to the ECJ to overturn the Decision as it considers that legislation should be drawn up under EU Environmental laws which come under 1st Pillar (EC Treaty) rather than the Framework Decision which was adopted under 3rd Pillar (TEU) which relates to justice and home affairs.

ENVIRONMENTAL ACTION PROGRAMMES

The Programmes have each concentrated on certain aspects of protecting the environment and last from 5–10 years. The first 4 programmes mainly concentrated on setting emission levels in relation to water, soil, air and waste pollution).

1st Environmental Action programme 1972–6).

It introduced the EEC's 11 environmental principles and set out targets to reduce pollution.

- Pollution is better prevented at source;
- In decision making processes, environmental effects should be taken into account as early as possible;
- Exploitation of natural resources to be avoided if they cause significant harm to the ecological balance;
- Scientific knowledge should be advanced to help in the protection of the environment;
- The polluter pays principle;
- Countries activities should not degrade the environments of others;
- The environmental policy of member states must take into account the interests of developing countries;
- The community should participate in international organisations to promote global environmental policy;
- Environmental education should be promoted throughout the community;
- Pollution control should be established at an all levels (from local, regional, national, community, international);
- National environmental policy to be harmonised within the community.

The 2nd Programme ran from 1977–1981, the 3rd from 1982–1986 and the 4th from 1987–1992.

The 5th Programme

'Towards sustainability' (from 1993–2000) saw a new approach with the introduction of sustainable development, preventive and precautionary measures.(see UK Government website on sustainable development: *www.sustainable-development.gov.uk*)

6th Environmental Action Programme

The European Commission adopted the 6th programme 'Environment 2010: Our Future, Our Choice' in 2001. It outlines the priorities for 2001-2010 and focuses on four priority areas:

1. **Climate change:** Includes global emission cuts 20–40 per cent by 2020.
2. **Nature and bio-diversity:** To reduce threats to the survival of many species and their habitats.
3. **The Environment and health:** Including water, air and noise strategies.
4. **Sustainable use of natural resources and waste:** Policies to increase recycling, and waste prevention objectives.

AREAS OF EU ENVIRONMENTAL LEGISLATION

Areas of EU Environmental legislation are categorised as:
General Provisions, Sustainable Development, Waste, Noise, Air, Water, Nature and Biodiversity, Soil Protection, Civil Protection (*e.g.* major accidents involving dangerous substances, *etc.*), Climate Change.

GENERAL PROVISIONS

1)Action Programmes

5th and 6th Environmental Action Programmes

2) Principles of Environmental policy

Precautionary Principle   The precautionary approach has been adopted in Art.174(2) (ex 130r) in respect of environmental protection, but does not yet compel member states to take a precautionary approach. See the *Duddridge* case in the English courts. In 2000 the Commission adopted a Communication on the Precautionary Principle.

Environmental Liability (the polluter pays)   A White Paper on Environmental Liability was adopted by the Commission in 2000. It set out the structure for a future EU environmental liability regime aimed at implementing the polluter pays principle to cover both 'traditional damage' (damage to persons and goods) and environmental damage. It recommended a strict liability regime for hazardous activities. In case of environmental damage, compensation to be paid by the polluter which should be spent on the restoration of damage. For cases concerning environmental damage, public interest groups should have rights when public bodies responsible for tackling environmental damage have not acted. Such public interest groups should also be allowed to take action in urgent cases if there is a need to prevent damage. A draft directive has been proposed by the European Commission.

3) Environmental Instruments

Environmental instruments includes measures such as environmental taxes, Eco labeling scheme, EMAS (Eco-Management and Audit Scheme), LIFE (Financial instrument for the environment), European Environment Agency, etc.

4) Application and control of community environmental law

The 1998 pan-European Aarhus Convention on Access to Information, Public Participation in Decision Making and Access to Justice in Environmental matters: The Commission is replacing the 1990 Freedom of Information Directive, with a more up-to-date Directive. It will also incorporate the terms of the Aarhus Treaty, ready for the EU to ratify at a later date.

Framework Decision on protecting the environment through criminal law: The Commission proposed a directive to protect the environment through criminal law but it failed to be adopted and instead a Framework Decision 2003 was adopted in 2003. The Commission has appealed to the ECJ against the decision to introduce a Framework Decision, adopted under Maastricht Treaty provisions, rather than a Directive adopted under environmental law provisions under Art.175 EC Treaty (see above). The Decision lists environmental offences which should be established as criminal offences under national criminal law. Details of specific environmental legislation (Directives, Regulations, etc.) and case law is included in other chapters. Visit the European Union On-line website, *http://europa.eu.int*, for comprehensive details of treaties, legislation and policies. It has on-line web assistance for enquiries. Another useful site is the European Environmental Law website: *www.eel.nl*.

BACKGROUND TO EU LEGISLATION

The European economic community (EEC) began as a common trading market of 6 countries in 1957 and was established with the Treaty of Rome. Since then (1957), the EEC has expanded, with more members, as well as developing more spheres of influence over policies of the member states. With its altering role, the EEC became the European Community (EC). The 1992 Maastricht Treaty (also referred to TEU) created the European Union (EU). The EU is not a legal personality, unlike the European Community. Art.5 (ex E) of TEU provides that the EU operates under or through the institutions of the European Community. Therefore, strictly speaking, it is EC or Community law rather than EU law. However, increasingly the EU UK Government refer to 'EU' law, *e.g.* EU Directives, etc. In 2003 there were 15 member countries; the UK joining in 1973. Under 'enlargement' a number of Central and Eastern European and Mediterranean countries are preparing to join the EU, with the first group, set to join in 2004. The Treaty of Amsterdam provides for institutional changes once there are at least 20 member states.

Relevant EU Institutions for law and policy

1) **The European Commission** is made up of Commissioners appointed from each state. One Commissioner has portfolio for the environment. The European Commission recommends most EU legislation and enforces it.

2) **European Courts of Justice (including Court of First Instance):** The European Court of Justice (ECJ) is the

ultimate authority for legal interpretation and EU legislation. The ECJ also incorporates the European Court of First Instance, which has a more limited jurisdiction. The Commission can take the governments of member states to the ECJ if they are not implementing EU law. (N.B. The European Court of Human Rights (ECHR), which includes the European Commission of Human Rights, is based on the European Convention on Human Rights and is not part of the EU courts).

3) **The Council of the European Union (was Council of Ministers):** The Council is where the interests of member states are represented. Environmental meetings are attended by Environmental Ministers.

4) **European Parliament:** The Parliament is made up of MEPs from the various member states.

5) **European Ombudsman:** The European Ombudsman investigates complaints about maladministration by institutions and bodies of the European Union.

EU Legislation

National law has to take into account EU law (both legislation and case law) and in situations of conflicting law, EU law prevails over national law. If UK legislation appears to be incompatible with EU law, provided the applicant has 'standing', it can be challenged through a judicial review in the domestic courts. This should not be confused with rights to challenge the validity of EU law in the ECJ under Art.230 EC treaty, provided the applicant has 'standing'.

EU law comprises of:

- **Primary Legislation**—Treaties
- **EU's international agreements**
- **Secondary Legislation**—Regulations, Directives, Decisions, etc.
- **Case Law**

1) Primary legislation Primary legislation, producing new treaties or amendments to existing treaties, is drawn up by agreement between the governments of the member states which then has to be ratified by the national parliaments. Treaties do not come into force until they have been ratified. The primary source of law is the Treaty of Rome 1957 (also referred to as EC Treaty). The EC Treaty has been amended by the Single European Act (SEA) 1986, Treaty of the European Union (TEU) 1992 (also known as the Maastricht Treaty), the Treaty of Amsterdam 1997 and the Treaty of Nice 2000. The Maastricht Treaty altered the name of the EEC to EC, to reflect changes in its activities and created European citizenship.

Articles within an EU treaty are similar to sections within an UK Act. The Amsterdam Treaty renumbered the articles of the EC Treaty and the Maastricht Treaty. Text will often give the original article number as well as the current number, *e.g.* Art.234 (ex 177). Articles are capable of having vertical and horizontal effect (see Direct Effect below).

2) International Agreements   The EU has co-operation or trading agreements with other countries. It is also party to some international treaties in its own right.

3) Secondary Legislation   Legislation normally starts with a proposal by the Commission and the Council of the EU make the decision, sometimes with input from Parliament. The European parliament has increasingly gained more influence in the drafting of legislation.

Art.249 (ex 189) provides the Council and Commission with powers to:

- **Make Regulations (not to be confused with UK Regulations)**
- Regulations have general application and are binding in their entirety and are directly applicable to all member states immediately. Regulations are capable of having vertical effect (against the member state) and horizontal effect (against an individual or organisation).
- **Issue Directives**—environmental law is mainly in the form of Directives which are then transposed into UK law through domestic legislation. Directives are capable of having vertical effect.
- **Take Decisions**—Decisions are binding in their entirety on whom they are addressed: specific member states or individuals or companies.
- **Make Recommendations and Opinions**—which have no binding force, but can be used a persuasive authority in national courts.

Directives   Require the member states to implement the EC law by changes in their national law. Under Art.250(ex 189) directives are binding in policy, but allow the individual member state to choose the form and method of implementation. It gives flexibility, but also gives rise for the possibility that the directive may not be being adequately transposed in national law or that states will not impose equal standards. In the UK, directives are implemented through an Act or delegated legislation (statutory instruments). Directives usually give a transition period for new legislation to be introduced, allowing for the gradual harmonisation by member states. If a member state fails to transpose a directive adequately in the time designated, then action may be taken by an individual to enforce the 'direct effect' of an directive. In English law, an individual can make a challenge through a judicial review.

4) Case Law   EU Case law includes judgments of the European Court of Justice (ECJ)and the European Court of First Instance. Cases included responses to referrals from the Commission, national courts of the member states or individuals.

Direct Effect (Vertical and Horizontal Effect)   Following *Van Gend en Loos* (1963), it was held that some provisions of EU law can be relied on directly by individuals in the Courts of Individual Member states, irrespective of the provisions made (or failed to be made) by the member state to implement the EU law. In *Van Gend en Loos*, the ECJ declared that EC law had direct effect if: the law was clear and unambiguous, it is unconditional and not dependent on the exercise of discretion and not dependent on further action by EC or member state, which would prevent directives from having direct effect (see *Duddridge* (1995) in English Courts, where Precautionary Principle was considered discretionary).

Vertical Effect means action can be taken against the member state in the national courts. Horizontal Effect means action can be taken against an individual/organisation in national courts. Articles and Regulations are capable of having vertical and horizontal effect, whereas Directives are capable of having vertical effect.

If it satisfies the conditions set down by *Van Gend en Loos*, EU law will have Vertical Effect. Action can be taken in respect of a Directive provided the implementation date has passed. Vertical Effect means that an individual can take a member state to court (the national court of that member state not the European Courts of Justice) to uphold obligations by public bodies or 'emanations of the State' arising from EU law.

The European Courts of Justice held that the applicant had a claim in the English Courts based on an unimplemented Directive, *Marshall v Southampton AHA* (1986). The question had been referred to ECJ by the English Court as an Art.177 reference (now Art.234). In a similar claim, in *Foster v British Gas* (1991), the House of Lords held that at the time British Gas had not been privatised and it was considered an emanation of the state. In comparison in *Duke v GEC Reliance Ltd* (1988), the House of Lords held that it was not possible to enforce the directive against an individual (or company) which is horizontal effect. *R. v Durham CC & others Ex p. Huddleston* (2002), the Court of Appeal held that the unimplemented Directive overruled national law, quashing the decision to allow planning permission for mineral extraction to be re-activated without a EIA.

Preliminary Ruling under Art.234 (ex. Art.177)   If during a hearing in the national court, the judge is unsure of the interpretation of EU law, then the case must be suspended whilst questions are referred to the ECJ for interpretation under Art.234. Once the ECJ has ruled on the matter, the national court then decide on the case, *e.g. Mayer Parry Case* (2003), where the English courts asked the ECJ to give an interpretation of the definition of waste.

Proportionality   Measures taken must be in proportion to the purpose to be attained, see *Commission v Denmark (Danish Bottles Case)* (1988). In *France v Commission (the PCP Case)* (1994), it was held that a member state can apply stricter standards, but has to prove they are necessary and proportionate. Both of these cases show how environmental laws can be connected with single market issues and must be proportionate.

The EU Courts (ECJ and European Court of First Instance)

As well as the main European Court of Justice, in 1988 a European Court of First Instance was created to help with the workload of the EJC and has jurisdiction over certain cases. Judges and Advocates-General are appointed to the courts. An Advocates-General prepare an analysis of a case and give recommendations, known as opinions, to the ECJ. The ECJ reaches a decision in private, so no dissenting judgments are given, although it may differ from the opinion of the Advocate-General. ECJ judgments do not contain *obiter dicta* or *ratio decidendi* as in English law. When a case comes before the EJC, there are complex rules governing who will hear the case. The European Court of First Instance can not hear preliminary rulings under Art.234 or cases against member states but can hear judicial reviews brought by *'natural or legal persons'*. Appeals may be made to the Court of First Instance on points of law only, not on points of fact, as can appeals from the court on to the ECJ.

JUDICIAL REMEDIES

1) Actions for Failure to fulfill treaty obligations under Art.226/7

The European Commission can investigates complaints it receives that a member state is in breach of its EU obligations. If the member state is found to be in breach, it is given the opportunity to rectify the situation. If it fails to do so, the Commission will issue the member state with a Reasoned Opinion. Should the Member state fail to comply with the opinion, the Commission has the discretion to commence legal proceeding, in the EJC, under Art.226 which can result in the ECJ issuing a fine against the member state. Under Art.227, a member state is able to take action against another member state.

2) Action for annulment under Art.230

Under Art.230 (ex 173) there are provisions for a judicial review to be made in respect of 'Acts' such as regulations, directives and decisions. Member states, the Council and Commission are privileged applicants and as such have automatic 'standing'. The European Parliament can bring an action in certain circumstances but does not have automatic rights. Cases brought by individuals (natural or legal persons, which includes environmental groups), are non-privileged applicants and have to prove standing, *i.e.* that the reviewable act is of direct and individual concern, and is heard in the Court of First Instance rather than ECJ. Greenpeace and local residents were not granted '*locus standi*' in *Stitching Greenpeace Council (Greenpeace Int.) v EC* (1998), but standing was relaxed in *Jego-Quere & Cie SA v Commission* (2002) as the ECJ stated the number and position of others affected was not relevant. If the individual(s) can not prove standing, a direct complaint can be made to the European Commission who may take action under Art.226.

3) Action for failure to act under Art.232

Under Art.232(ex 175) applicants to apply for declaration that an institution has infringed the Treaty by failing to act.

4) Actions for Damages under Arts 235 and 288

A successful applicant can seek damages, under Arts 235 or 288.

5) Actions by Community Staff Under Art.236

Community staff can take action in relation to employment rights.

6) Referrals to ECJ for preliminary rulings under Art.234

---

8. POLLUTION CONTROL (INCLUDING IPC AND PPC)

Historically, early legislation to control pollution was introduced in the 19th century through the Public Health Acts and the Alkali Inspectorate and, was formed to give advice to the emerging chemicals industries. The Alkali, etc. Work Regulations 1906 dealt with noxious fumes, whereas Clear Air Act 1956 and 1968, gave power to LAs to control smoke. The Health and Safety Executive was formed in 1974 to deal with all aspects of health, safety and welfare at work, to include responsibility for the Alkali Inspectorate (later the Industrial Air Pollution Inspectorate). By the 1970's, control of pollution was fragmented, dealt with by various authorities, sometimes with overlapping responsibilities. In 1976, the RCEP in its 5th Report, acknowledged that an integrated approach was needed and proposed that one body should regulate the release of prescribed substances to allow an assessment to be made of the impact the releases have on the environment as a whole. Gradually a more unified approach was adopted, with the establishment of Her Majesty's Inspectorate of Pollution (HMIP) in 1987, the National Rivers Authority (NRA) in 1989 and Waste Regulatory Authorities (WRA) set up by part II of Environmental Protection Act 1990. An integrated approach to pollution control, IPC regime, was introduced through Part I EPA 1990, which is now being superseded by an integrated pollution prevention and control regime introduced by Pollution, Prevention and Control Act 1999. Pollution control continued to be regulated by the 3 different authorities, HMIP, NRA and WRA, until they were amalgamated into the Environment Agency in 1996 following the Environment Act 1995.

PRIMARY LEGISLATION FOR POLLUTION CONTROL

Environmental Protection Act 1990 (amended by EA 1995)

- **Part I Integrated Pollution Control (IPC) and Local Air Pollution Control (LAPC).** Gradually being replaced by Pollution Prevention and Control Act 1999.
- **Part II Waste on Land:** Waste Regulatory Authorities set up. The Introduction of Duty of Care, etc. in respect of any person who imports, produces, carries, keeps, treats, or disposes of controlled waste, or as a broker has control of such waste.
- **Part IIA Contaminated Land:** makes provision for polluted land.
- **Part III Statutory Nuisances and Clean Air:** Sections 79–82 replaced Public Health Act 1936 and Public Health (reoccurring nuisance) Act 1969.
- **Part VII Nature Conservation in Great Britain and Countryside Matters in Wales:** Creation of new nature conservancy councils.
- **Part IX General Power to give effect to Community and other international obligations, etc.:** Allows Secretary of State to introduce regulations.

Environment Act 1995

- **Part I:** For a more unified approach to dealing with pollution, the Environment Agency was incorporated from HMIP, NRA and WRA.

- **Part II Contaminated Land and Mines:** Part llA Contaminated Land ss.78A–78YC was inserted into EPA 1990.
- **Part III:** Creation of National Park authorities.
- **Part IV Air Quality:** Introduced Air Quality Strategy and Air Quality Management Areas.
- **Part V Waste:** Amended Waste definitions to s.75 of the EPA 1990.

Pollution Prevention and Control Act 1999 (PPCA 1999)

PPCA 1999 is replacing IPC/LAPC under Part I EPA 1990, with a Pollution Prevention and Control Regime (PPC) (see below).

Other important legislation includes: Water Industry Act 1991 and 1999, Water Resources Act 1991, Clean Air Act 1993, Noise and Statutory Nuisance Act 1993, Noise Act 1996 and Control of Pollution Act 1974 (noise).

This chapter deals with IPC/LAPC and PPC (IPPC and LAPPC) in detail, other chapters specifically deal with statutory nuisance, water pollution, air pollution, noise, waste management and contaminated land.

Legal Definition of terms used to describe 'best means'

BPM—Best Practicable Means is an non-technical term used a defence to statutory nuisance under s.80(70) of the **EPA** 1990.

BATNEEC—Best Available Techniques Not Exceeding Excessive Costs is used in IPC regime for individual processes, s.7(4) of the EPA 1990.

BPEO—Best Practicable Environmental Option. If a process releases substances into more than one medium (land, air or water), then BPEO approach is adopted rather than BATNEEC under IPC regime.

BAT—Best Available Techniques is used in the new PPC Regime.

INTEGRATED POLLUTION CONTROL (IPC)

Integrated Pollution Control was introduced through Part I of EPA 1990. It is now gradually being replaced by PPC regime being introduced through PPCA 1999. IPC (Integrated Pollution Control) authorisations will continue to operate until the operator has to apply for a new permit under PPC regulations. IPC regulates emissions to land, water and air, taking into account that when a pollutant is discharged, it may enter more than one environmental medium (land, air or water) and that solving one pollution problem may create another. IPC deals with the potentially most polluting industries or technologically complex processes in England and Wales and is regulated by the Environment Agency.

IPC authorisation

Under s.6 of the EPA 1990, prior authorisation was required from the Environment Agency before certain processes could be carried on or certain prescribed substances be discharged into the environment as specified in the amended Environmental Protection (Prescribed Processes & Substances) Regulations 1991. The application had to consider the overall impact of all emissions into air, water and land. In *HMIP v Safety Kleen Ltd* (1994), the magistrates court decided that the storing of a substance in a tanker could be a 'process', if it was capable of causing pollution.

Conditions of authorisation

Section 7 of the EPA 1990 required the Environment Agency to make conditions for the authorisation and ensure the BATNEEC/BPEO were used.

If the process released emissions into one environmental medium, then BATNEEC applied and if more than one medium used, the operator had to use BPEO, to achieve the best environmental solution and least impact on environment overall. Section 7(11) gave the Secretary of State powers to direct the Environment Agency on authorisation and conditions to be included in authorisation.

The Court of Appeal held that a regulator could still refuse to issue an authorisation if an emission is harmful, even if BATNEEC was applied. In *Gateshead Metropolitan BC v Secretary of State for the Environment and Northumbria Water* (1995), it was held that if HMIP concluded that BATNEEC would not achieve the results required by s.7(2) and s.7(4) of EPA 1990, it may be proper to refuse an authorisation. The Court of Appeal held that a neighbour had sufficient interest to apply for a judicial review in *R. v Bolton MBC Ex p. Kirkman* (1998), but the LA was right to pay heed to the BPEO, in respect of planning permission for a waste incinerator.

Section 15 of the EPA 1990 provided for an operator to appeal against the decision of Environment Agency to refuse to issue or vary an authorisation or the conditions of the authorisation. Operators with existing IPC authorisations have to monitor their emissions and report annually to the Environment Agency.

Breach of Authorisation Conditions

If the Environment Agency believes that an operator is breaching the conditions of his authorisation, it can serve either a:

- Notice to Revoke Authorisation,
- Enforcement Notice; or
- Prohibition Notice, is served to suspend an authorisation if regulator believes that an operation is in imminent risk of serious pollution.

The Operator can appeal against the issue of one of these notices.

LOCAL AIR POLLUTION CONTROL (LAPC)

LAPC is a regime for the control of air emissions from less polluting substances and was introduced under Part 1 of EPA 1990 and enforced by LAs (district/borough councils and some port health authorities). Following the PPCA 1999, LAPC is being replaced by Local Air Pollution Prevention and Control (LAPPC).

Enforcement

Criminal offences under IPC/LAPC include operating a process without an authorisation, failing to comply with a condition of an authorisation or an Enforcement or Prohibition Notice. Depending on the offence, on summary conviction, the penalty is a fine of up to £20,000 and/or a prison sentence and on indictment an unlimited fine and/or up to 5 years in prison. Section 157 of the EPA 1990 provides that corporate bodies can be held liable for criminal offences committed under the Act and directors, managers and other senior officers can be held personally liable as well.

Public registers

Section 20 of the EPA 1990 requires the Environment Agency and LAs to maintain details of IPC and LAPC applications and authorisations on public registers. The Secretary of State has powers to allow information to be left off the register in the interest of over national security under s.21. Operators can apply to the Environment Agency to have information withheld under s.22 on the grounds of commercial confidentiality.

Statutory Nuisance and IPC/LAPC

LAs can not act under statutory nuisance, s.79 of the EPA 1990, to abate a nuisance which is covered under Part 1 of EPA 1990. However, this does not prevent an individual from taking action under s.82 of the EPA 1990.

POLLUTION PREVENTION AND CONTROL (PPC)

The 1996 EU Directive on Integrated Pollution Prevention and Control, which adopts an integrated pollution prevention and control regime, was introduced into domestic law through the PPCA 1999. PPCA 1999 is the enabling Act with the specific legislation being contained in the Pollution Prevention and Control (England and Wales) Regulations 2000 (referred to as PPC Regulations 2000). Pollution Prevention and Control (PPC) will eventually replace existing legislation under Part 1 EPA 1990.

Operators can continue under their existing IPC/LAPC licences until their industrial sector is phased in. Operators either setting up new installations or existing operations with substantial changes, which will have a significant negative effect on human beings or the environment, will have to apply for an PPC (either IPPC or LAPPC) permit under new Regulations. The new regime should be totally implemented by 2007.

What activities will be subject to PPC Regulations

PPC will take a wider range of environmental impacts into account than the current system of IPC. As well as considering land, water and air, it will include waste avoidance or minimisation, energy efficiency accident avoidance and minimisation of noise, odour, heat and vibration. PPC will apply to a wider range of industries than IPC.

Sch.1 PPC regulations 2000 lists activities which are subject to PPC regulations a) Energy industry; b) Chemical industry; c) Metal production and processing industries; d) Minerals industry; e) Waste management industry; f) Other activities. Activities will include:

a) All installations that are currently regulated under IPC.
b) Some installations currently under LAPC.
c) Some other installations not currently under IPC/LAPC. such as: landfill sites, intensive agriculture, large pig and poultry units, food & drink manufacturers.

Annex 1 of IPPC Directive contains details for thresholds (activities falling below the threshold are excluded, for example small landfill sites). PPC regulated industries are referred to as 'installations', whereas IPC regulated industries are referred to as 'processes'. This represents a more integrated approach, an installation has to be processed rather than individual processes within the installation.

Responsibilities of the Regulators

Part A   refers to the Integrated Polluting regime.
1) Part A1 Installations regulated by the Environment Agency. Covers emissions to air, land and water of the potentially more polluting processes. Mainly Part A of the old IPC regime plus waste disposal, food and farming.
2) Part A2 Installations (also known as LA-IPPC) are regulated by LAs although the Environment Agency has a supervisory role in respect of discharges into water. Covers emissions to air, land and water of processes with a lesser potential to pollute. Permits will not include waste, which will continue to be licensed separately. Part A2 installations have been added as an additional category of processes.

Part B installations   Covers same installations as covered by LAPC. Deals with local air pollution under PPCA 1999. The LA is responsibility for Part B installations activities, which previously came under LAPC.

Applying for PPC permit

Operators have to apply for a permit from the regulator (either Environment Agency or LA) prior to operation. Copies of the application will be placed on a public register and the public are able to submit comments during the consultation process. Statutory Consultees, as outlined in Reg.9 of PPC regulations 1999, are also consulted prior to the application being considered. The application can be granted subject to conditions or rejected and the operator has 6 months in which to appeal to the Secretary of State against a refusal to issue a permit or the conditions imposed.

Conditions

Sch.5 of PPC Regulations 2000 provides a list of the main polluting substances which have taken into account when fixing emission limits for conditions of the permit. Sch.4, Regs 7 and 10 of PPC Regulations 2000 provide the information required with an application. The regulator has to ensure that BAT is applied, that no significant pollution is caused and the risk of accidents and their consequences is minimised, impact of waste is minimised and energy is used efficiently.

The operator has to apply BAT to his operation and this is considered by the regulator when deciding whether to grant a permit. BATNEEC/BPEO definitions were introduced into UK law following UK Government policies, however, BAT is derived from the EC Directive. Reg.3 defines BAT as 'the most effective and advanced stage in the development of activities and their methods of operation which indicates the practical suitability of particular techniques for providing the basis for emission limit values designed to prevent and where that is not practicable, generally to reduce the emissions and the impact on the environment as a whole'. BAT refers to both the technology and the way in which the installation is operated. BAT takes into account the costs of the measures and the benefits in terms of preventing environmental damage.

The Secretary of State has the power to call in an application under Sch.4 para.14 and direct the regulator on the decision regarding a permit after holding a public enquiry or informal hearing.

Once a permit is issued, the regulator (either Environment Agency or LA) has to monitor emissions. The Environment Agency carries out a risk assessment to determine how frequently an installation has to be monitored. Operators also have to monitor emissions and send reports to the regulator.

Public Registers

Public registers have to been maintained by the regulator under Reg.29 PPC Regulations 2000. The Secretary of State has powers to allow information to be left off the register in the interest of national security under Reg.30. Operators may apply to the Environment Agency to have information withheld under Reg.31 on the grounds of commercial confidentiality. If the Environment Agency fails to make a determination within 14 days, the information is deemed to be commercially confidential by default.

Breach of Permit Conditions

Under Reg.23 of PPC Regulations 2000, the regulator (either the Environment Agency or LA) has a duty to supervise authorised activities and take necessary steps to ensure the operator is complying with the conditions of his permit.

- Enforcement Notice under Reg.24.
- Renovation Notice under Reg.21.
- Suspension Notice under Reg.25
- Variation Notice, under Reg.17.

The regulator must serve a Suspension Notice, if he considers there is imminent risk of serious injury. Operators have 2 months in which to make an appeal to the Secretary of State against a Notice being served.

Enforcement

The regulators are able to enforce PPC legislation through criminal law. It is Criminal offence to:

- Operate a PPC installation without a permit.
- Breach permit conditions.
- Fail to give notice of a permit transfer.
- Fail to comply with an Enforcement Notice or Suspension. Notice (issued by the Regulator).
- Intentionally make false entries on official records.

Reg.32 of the PPC regulations 2000 lists the offences and penalties under the PPC regime. For some offences the maximum penalty on summary conviction is a fine of up to £20,000 and if the sentencing is made in the Crown Court, an unlimited fine and/or prison sentence of up to 2 years. For other offences, on summary conviction a fine of up to £20,000 and up to 6 months in prison or both, and on indictment, a fine or up to 5 years in prison, or both. Corporate bodies can be held liable for offences, and directors, managers and other senior officers can be personally liable.

PPC and other legislation

IPPC overlaps with some other regulatory regimes. IPPC will gradually take over consents to discharge into controlled waters. IPPC permits must take into account Groundwater Regulations 1998. Under the Water Industry Act 1991, an operator who wishes to discharge trade effluent into sewers has to obtain a consent from the statutory sewerage undertaker. As some IPPC permits will include discharges into sewers, there will be some overlap of the regulatory regimes. IPPC has no overlap with contaminated land under Part IIA EPA 1990, although the standard of clean up required by the PPC regime, prior to the start of permitted activities, is to a higher standard then required by Part IIA. With regards to waste, an EU landfill directive is being introduced and brings the larger landfill sites under IPPC.

Statutory Nuisance

LAs can only take action against a PPC installation under s.79 of the EPA 1990 if the nuisance is not covered by the conditions of a permit, although this does not prevent an individual from taking action under s.82.

Planning permission, permitted development rights and EIA

The development of land by an operator is controlled both by the requirement to obtain planning permission and a permit for emissions. Developers can apply for planning permission and a PPC permit in parallel. Sometimes, they will delay applying for permit, until the outcome of planning permission is known.

Certain waste installations need planning permission, before a permit can be issued. If a proposed development comes within permitted development rights, it does not require planning permission, unless it requires an environmental impact assessment under Sch.1 or 2 of The Town and Country Planning (EIA) (E&W) Regulations 1999. In *R v Wirral MBC Ex p. Gray* (1998), it was held that further development of a chemical plant which came under permitted development rights would only need planning permission if the development came with Schs 1 or 2 of the EIA Regulations 1999.

The Environment Agency has issued pollution prevention and guidance notes on a range of pollutants for various industrial sectors/activities *www.environment-agency.gov.uk*. The Department of the Environment, Food and Rural Affairs has also issued a Practical Guide on IPPC: *www.defra.gov.uk*.

9. STATUTORY NUISANCE

Statutory Nuisance controls matters which are 'a nuisance or prejudicial to health' and originates from the Public Health Act 1936, designed to protect public health. It has now been incorporated into legislation to protect the environment: Part lll of the Environmental Protection Act 1990 (EPA 1990) regulates 'Statutory Nuisances & Clean Air'. Statutory nuisance is regulated by the local authority (LA) although if the LA fails to act, an 'aggrieved person' has the right to apply to the magistrates court for the nuisance to be abated.

Matters dealt with by other regulatory regimes

Certain types of pollution are dealt with by other regulatory regimes and are specifically excluded from statutory nuisance.

- Land in a 'contaminated state' is excluded, s.79(1)A of the EPA 1990. However, the definition for 'contaminated state' under s.79(1)B differs from 'contaminated land' under Part IIA of the EPA 1990, which means that not all contaminated land excluded from the Statutory Nuisance will fall under the contaminated land regime.

- Smoke covered by of the Clean Air Act 1993 is excluded, s.79(3) of the EPA 1990.
- Emissions regulated by the IPC/LAPC regime under part 1 of the EPA 1990 or the incoming PPC regime introduced by PPCA 1999 are excluded. This does not prevent an 'aggrieved person' being able to take action under s.82 .

Statutory nuisance regulated by local authority(LA)

Under s.79(1) of the EPA 1990 the LA has a duty to inspect its area and to investigate complaints of nuisance. The LA's duties are normally undertaken by Environmental Health Officers. As with common law nuisance, certain factors have to be considered when deciding if a matter is a statutory nuisance. These include:

- the location and the nature of the matter. In *Sturges v Bridgman* (1879), the court stated, 'what would be a nuisance in Belgrave Square would not necessarily be so in Bermondsey'.
- the time, duration and frequency of the matter.
- the utility of the activity causing the alleged nuisance.

Although it is an offence not to comply with an abatement notice, the LA only has to decide on the balance of probabilities that a nuisance exists. If a LA is satisfied a statutory nuisance exists or is likely to occur, then under s.80, it must take steps to abate the nuisance. It was held in *R. v Carrick DC Ex p. Shelley* (1996) that the LA failed in its duty by only observing and not acting upon pollution of local beaches. The LA has to serve an abatement notice on the person responsible for the creating the nuisance. If a LA fails to take action, the Secretary of State has the powers to take action under Sch.3 of the EPA 1990; an 'aggrieved person' can also take action under s.82.

What Constitutes statutory nuisance

Section 79(1)(a)–(g) of the EPA 1990 lists matters which constitute a statutory nuisance if they are prejudicial to health or a nuisance, which includes the state of premises, smoke, gases, fumes, dust, smells, other effluvia, animals, noise from premises and noise in the street. Section 79(1)(h) provides for other matters to be declared a statutory nuisance.

a) **Any premises in such a state as to be prejudicial to health or a nuisance.** Section 79(7) defines premises as land, building or vessel. In recent years, there has been an increase in the number of cases taken by tenants under s.82, in an attempt to improve their living conditions. The court held that sewers were not 'premises' within the meaning of s.79(1a) of the EPA 1990, in *East Riding of Yorkshire Council v Yorkshire Water* (2000). However, in *Hounslow LBC v Thames Water* (2003), the High Court held that sewage treatment works did constitute 'premises' under s.79(1)(d) when read with s.79(7). The court held that condensation and its associated mould growth could make premises prejudicial to health in *GLC v Tower Hamlets LBC* (1984). In *Cunningham v Birmingham CC* (1998), the Divisional court held that the Magistrates Court was wrong in determining the case by relating the council's duties to the particular family health requirements. The House of Lords held that older property, with inadequate lavatory facilities, was not a statutory nuisance in *Oakley v Birmingham CC* (2000). In *Southwark LBC v Ince* (1989), it was held that train noise in property due to inadequate insulation against noise was deemed to be prejudicial to health and was a statutory nuisance. The Court allowed an appeal by the LA in Haringey *LBC v Jowett* (1999) against conviction under s.79(1a) that premises with inadequate sound insulation from traffic were prejudicial health on the grounds that s.79(6a) precluded noise from external traffic. In *Baxter v Camden LBC (No.2)* (1999), a tenant sued her LA landlord in **private nuisance** for inadequate soundproofing of her flat. The House of Lords dismissed claim, as the LA had not authorised any nuisance. Although the case concerned (private) nuisance not statutory nuisance, it would be considered *'persuasive precedent'*.

b) **Smoke emitted from premises so as to be prejudicial to health or a nuisance.** Smoke controlled by the Clean Air Act 1993 is not included as a statutory nuisance. Section 79 (3) provides that s.79 (1b) does not apply to smoke emitted from a private dwelling within a smoke control area, dark smoke from a chimney of a building or furnace of a boiler or other industrial or trade premises or smoke from railway steam engine. In *Griffiths v Pembrokeshire CC* (2000) it was held that smoke could constitute a nuisance on the basis of the smell of smoke alone and it was not necessary to prove the presence of visible smoke.

c) **Fumes or gases emitted from premises so as to be prejudicial to health or a nuisance.** Section 79(1c) only applies to private dwellings. 'Fumes' means any airborne solid matter smaller than dust and 'gases' and includes vapour and moisture precipitated from vapour, s.79(7). Section 79(C) could apply to circumstances when crop spraying drifts over neighbouring properties. Section 79(C) would apply to someone causing a nuisance with other types of spraying, provided the activities was not covered by IPC/ PPC regimes, however, this would not prevent an 'aggrieved person' taking action under s.82.

d) **any dust, steam, smell or other effluvia arising on industrial, trade or business premises and being prejudicial to health or a nuisance.** Section 79(1d) does not apply to steam emitted from railway engines, Section 79(3). 'Dust' does not include dust emitted from a chimney as an ingredient of smoke s.79(7). However, in *Hounslow LBC v Thames Water* (2003), the High Court held that sewage treatment works did constitute 'premises' under s.79(d) read with s.79(7).

e) **any accumulation or deposit which is prejudicial to health or a nuisance.** It was held in *Coventry CC v Cartwright* (1975) that an accumulation of inert matter, scrap iron, broken glass or tin cans did not extend to 'cause physical injury'. However, it could be argued that such an accumulation might encourage vermin, although there is also the Prevention of damage by Pest Act 1949.

f) **any animal kept in such a place or manner as to be prejudicial to health or a nuisance.**

g) **noise emitted from premises so as to be prejudicial to health or a nuisance.** Section 79(1g) does not apply to aircraft apart from model aircraft, s.79(36). 'Noise' includes vibration, s.79(7). In a test case, residents in Cumbria are taking action under s.82 in respect of noise from wind turbines. They have issued summons against Powergen Renewables (the Energy Co), Windprospect Ltd (the Wind Farm Co) and Cockermouth and Barrow BC; a trial date has been set for early 2004.

ga) noise emitted from or caused by vehicle, machinery or equipment in a street (amended by Noise and Statutory Nuisance Act 1993). Section 79(1ga) does not apply to noise made by traffic, any naval, military or air force, s.79(6A).

h) Any other matter declared by enactment to be a statutory nuisance.

Some matters not included in Statutory Nuisance

Statutory nuisance does not seem to cover all environmental harm. *e.g.*

- **light pollution** includes lighting from security lighting, floodlights, etc. Campaign groups are calling for light pollution to be included in statutory nuisance legislation.
- **shadow flicker** from wind turbines.
- **Ionising and Non-ionising Radiation.** Non-ionising radiation includes electromagnetic radiation, also known as EMFs or electrosmog, and is given off by power stations, power lines, telecommunication transmitters, including TETRA police radio masts, mobile phone masts and mobile phones. Ionising radiation is emitted by natural sources (*e.g.* radon gas and cosmic rays) and man-made sources (*e.g.* atomic bomb fallout, radioactive waste and includes nuclear waste and x-rays). Regulators are responsible for the discharge levels of both ionising and non-ionising radiation from installations. However, there is no provision for an individual to take action under s.79.

Statutory nuisance does not seem to specifically make provision for energy, including heat or radioactivity or light or other electromagnetic radiation. Exposure to light, shadow flicker or radiation might be considered 'an accumulation or deposit' under s.79(1)E. Wind Turbines can be up to 400 feet high and campaigners have expressed concerns about the public's risk from turbine blades detaching or disintegrating, and in cold weather, ice being flung off blades when the wind gets up. If a wind turbine did become unsafe, then possibly action could be taken under s.79(a) or (e). Even if an individual is unable to take action in statutory nuisance, it would not prevent him from taking action in (private) nuisance.

What constitutes a 'nuisance' or 'prejudicial to health'

A matter only has to be a nuisance or prejudicial to health, not both, as affirmed by *Betts v Penge* (1942). Section 79(7c) defines 'prejudicial to health as meaning injurious, or likely to cause injury to health In *Oakley v Birmingham CC* (2001), the House of Lords interpreted the meaning of 'prejudicial to health' in s.79, and in so doing, considered the background to the legislation. The court found the purpose of the section was to deal with conditions, such as dampness, excessive dirt or rat infestation, that posed a risk to health. In *Southwark LBC v Simpson* (1999) it was held considering whether a matter was likely to be injurious to health, the expert witness need not be medically qualified but should have some experience or expertise in that area.

The court considered the meaning of nuisance in *National Coal Board v Neath BC* (1976) and held that statutory nuisance had the same meaning as in public or private nuisance. In *Wivenhoe Port v Colchester BC* (1985), the Crown Court held that dust was not a nuisance within the definition of statutory nuisance as it must interfere materially with the personal comfort of residents in so much as it affected their well-being although not necessarily prejudicial to their health (case taken prior to EPA 1990). However, in *Godfrey v Conway CBC* (2000), it was held that the test to establish statutory nuisance was the same as private nuisance at common law, that is whether the nuisance constituted an unreasonable interference with the use and enjoyment of the complainant's land.

The form of the abatement notice

The LA can issue a notice under s.80(1a) requiring the nuisance to be abated, or prohibit or restrict its reoccurrence under s.80(1b) requiring execution of such works or other steps as necessary to comply with the abatement notice. The notice gives a time limit for compliance with the notice. In *Kirkless MBC v Field* (1998), the Court of Appeal held that the abatement notice was invalid as it did not specify how the nuisance was to be abated. *Kirkless* was overruled by the Court of Appeal in *R. v Falmouth and Truro Port Authority Ex p. South West Water* (2000) when it was held that the LA could state the means by which the nuisance was abated to the perpetrator, if the LA prescribed the way the nuisance was to be abated, then that method must be employed. It was held in *Cambridge CC v Douglas* (2000), that the LA did not have to specify the source of the statutory nuisance in the abatement notice, as it was not a matter within the LA's knowledge. The Court of Appeal held that the facts relating to issuing abatement notices are to be assessed on circumstances at the date the notice was issued, not the date of the court hearing, *Surrey Free Inns PLC v Gosport BC* (1999). In an appeal to the High Court, it was held that once an abatement notice is issued, it remains in force indefinitely unless otherwise stated, *Wellington DC v Gordon* (1991).

Who is responsible for the nuisance?

- Normally an abatement notice served on the person responsible for statutory nuisance. If more than one person is responsible for nuisance, the notice can be served on each person responsible.
- If the person responsible can not be found, or the nuisance has yet to occur, notice can be served on the owner/occupier of the premises.
- If nuisance relates to vehicle or machinery or equipment, person responsible is the driver or operator.
- Where the nuisance arises from structural defect in premises, it is served on the owner of the premises. In *Network Housing Association Ltd v Westminster CC* (1995), it was held that not having noise insulation between adjoining council flats was the fault of the owner of the premises (the housing association) not the person making the noise.

Defences for non-compliance, including BPM

Any person who fails to comply with the abatement notice without reasonable excuse is guilty of an offence under s.80(4) and the reasonable excuse has to relate to difficulties met when trying to comply with the order. Section 80(7) provides for a defence of Best Practicable Means (BPM) for certain categories of statutory nuisance:

- Section 79(1)(a)(d)(e)(f) and (g) for nuisance caused by industrial, trade or business premises.
- Section 79(1)(ga) for noise emitted for industrial, trade or business purposes.
- Section 79(1)(b) for smoke emitted from chimneys (only).

Section 79(9) gives the full interpretation of BPM which includes 'practicable' meaning taking into account the local conditions and circumstances, and current technical knowledge and financial implications. Means to be employed includes design, installation and manner and periods of operation of plant or machinery and the design, construction and maintenance of buildings and structures.

Rights of appeal against abatement notice

Under s.80(3) the person served with the abatement notice has 21 days to appeal against the notice to the Magistrates Court. In some circumstances, a notice may be suspended pending the outcome of appeal, if compliance with the abatement notice would require expenditure before the appeal. Grounds for appeal in Reg.2(2) of Statutory Nuisance (Appeals) Regulations 1995 include:

- The abatement notice is not justified by Section 80 of the EPA 1990. In *Budd v Colchester BC* (1997), the LA had to justify the abatement notice.
- more time is needed to abate nuisance.
- Under s.80(7) use of BPM to abate nuisance is a defence.
- noise cases where the noise is covered by other legislation or notices cover noise.
- the abatement notice should have been served on another person other than the appellant.

On hearing the appeal, the Court may:

- quash the abatement notice.
- vary the abatement notice, including correcting a defect in the notice.
- dismiss the appeal.
- make an order for works to be carried out and contribution to be made by any person towards the cost of works.
- make an order regarding costs that LA can recover from appellant and any other person towards their expenses.

An Appeal on the facts can be made to the Crown Court within 21 days of the Magistrates Court hearing.

Non-compliance with abatement notice

Non-compliance with abatement notice is an offence under s80(4) EPA 1990 and there are several causes of action the LA can take.

a) **The LA can abate the nuisance themselves and recover costs.** As well as occasions when a person refuses to comply with an abatement notice, the LA may act when prompt action is required.

b) **Commence summary proceedings in the Magistrates Court for failure to comply with the notice.** It is a criminal offence to fail to comply with an abatement notice, s.80(4), and the standard of proof required is that of criminal law. The maximum penalty imposed by the court on industrial, trade, or business premises is £20,000, although there is no daily fine for continued non-compliance with the notice. For other premises, the levels of fines are less: the maximum penalty is £5000 and £500 for each day of non-compliance after the conviction. In *Botross v Hammersmith & Fulham LBC* (1994) it was held that statutory nuisance proceedings were criminal proceedings and compensation may be awarded by Court. When costs are due from a person who is the owner of the premises mentioned in the abatement notice, s.81(a) allows the LA to recover costs by making a land charge on the premises.

c) **Take proceedings in the High Court if a) and b) will not provide sufficient remedy.** Action can be taken in High Court for an injunction to secure abatement prohibition. Failing to comply with injunction can result in prison sentence. In *Bristol CC v Huggins* (1995), the defendant was sent to prison for 3 months for breaching an injunction obtained by LA after prosecutions under EPA 1990 failed.

Action in statutory nuisance by individual under s.82

Section 82 allows an aggrieved person to take action directly to the Magistrates Court, if the LA fail to act. The aggrieved person has to be affected by alleged nuisance but does not have to have a legal interest in the land, *AG(Gambia) v N'jie* (1961). An aggrieved person can only take action if the nuisance already exists, unlike the LA who can take preventive action against an anticipated nuisance. Under s.82 (7), the aggrieved person has to serve notice on the person responsible for the nuisance (the defendant), that he intends to take proceeding in the magistrates court. 3 days notice is required for noise nuisance and 21 days for any other type of nuisance. Under s.82(2) magistrates have to be satisfied that the alleged nuisance exists or if abated, is likely to reoccur and if so, can order either or both:

a) the defendant abates the nuisance within a specified time and executes any works necessary for that purpose:

b) Prohibit a re-occurrence of the nuisance and require the defendant to execute any works, within a specified time, to prevent a reoccurrence and may also impose a fine not exceeding level 5 (£5000).

If the person convicted under s.82(2) fails to comply with the magistrates' Order, then under s.82(8) he is liable to a fine of up to £5000 plus £500 for every day the Order is not complied with.

Section 82(4) defines whom proceedings can be brought against; usually the person who is responsible for the nuisance, if that person can not be found, then the occupier or the owner of the premises is held responsible. The owner is responsible in the case of defective premises. If the convicted person does not abate the nuisance or no person responsible can be found, magistrates can order the relevant LA, after having given it the opportunity to be heard, to take steps to abate the nuisance.

As with proceedings brought by the LA, where a nuisance has arisen from trade, industrial or business premises, it is a defence to show that BPM have been used to reduce the effects of nuisance.

Judicial Review of decisions relating to statutory nuisance

The decision of a LA not to take action under statutory nuisance can be challenged by judicial review. In *R(Anne) v Test Valley BC* (2002), the court held that the LA's decision not to take action under statutory nuisance could not be categorised as irrational or Wednesbury unreasonable. The aggrieved person could also have applied to the magistrates court to abate the nuisance under s.82.

---

10.   WATER POLLUTION

Good quality freshwater is essential for human health, both for drinking water and other human activities. Good quality freshwater is also needed in rivers, streams, etc. for plant life, fish and animals. Once water has been used, it is discharged back into receiving waters as effluent. Water pollution can be caused by various sources including waste, sewage and the water industry, commercial and domestic premises, educational and healthcare premises, run off from agriculture land. Pollutants need not necessarily be toxic substances, milk is very polluting to water. Pollutants can enter surface or groundwater directly from a point source, such as discharge from pipe or from a diffuse source, such as run off from agriculture land, urban storm drains or deposited from the atmosphere.

EU Policy

The EU has introduced a number of directives relating to standards for emissions and water quality which have been transposed into UK law. The Dangerous Substances in Water Directive 1976, with a Black list of substances to be eliminated from discharges and a Grey List of substances to be reduced. Daughter directives are being introduced for specific substances with set emission standards for discharge consents. Other Directives include: The Protection of Groundwater against Pollution caused by Certain Dangerous Substances Directive 1980, Nitrates Directive 1991, Urban Waste Water Treatment Directive 1991, Bathing Water Directive 1976, Drinking Water Directives 1980 and 1998 and Water Framework Directive 2000.

Government Policy

Early legislation to prevent and control pollution was introduced in the mid 19th century, with general public health acts, the Salmon Fisheries Act 1861 and the Rivers Pollution Prevention Act 1876. The 1876 act was replaced by the River (prevention of pollution) Act 1951 (extended by 1961 Act) which introduced the first system of discharge consents. Both the 1951 and 1961 Acts were replaced by the Control of Pollution Act 1974, which was replaced by Part III of the Water Resources Act 1991.

The Water Act 1989 restructured the water industry, both water supply and sewerage services and set up the National Rivers Authority (NRA) to regulate water supply and pollution. The provisions of the Water Act 1989 was consolidated in the Water Resources Act 1991 (WRA 1991) and Water Industry Act 1991 (WIA 1991). Water supplies and sewerage services are now run by privatised water companies, but they still remain statutory water and sewerage undertakers (some of the smaller companies supply water only). Following the Environment Act 1995, the

NRA was amalgamated into the Environment Agency who now regulate the water regime.

The Government is transposing in UK law the EU Water Framework Directive 2000 which requires member states to ensure 'good status' of all inland and coastal waters by 2015. The new regime will be regulated by the Environment Agency through River Basin Management Plans.

WATER REGIME

The main legislation to control water pollution is the WRA 1991 and WIA 1991 (with 1999 Act). WIA 1991 deals mainly with sewerage undertakers and discharges into sewers. WRA 1991 deals with water quality, pollution offences and prevention of pollution. The Environment Agency regulates water supply (drinking water quality), the quality of controlled waters and sewage treatment. Under s.108 of the EA 1995, the Environment Agency has powers of entry to carry out inspections and take water or effluent samples.

Controlled Waters

Section 82–4 of the WRA 1991 provides a system to introduce water quality standards (from EU Directives) for controlled waters. The water regime protects discharges into 'controlled waters', which are defined under s.104 of the WRA 1991:

a) relevant territorial waters, within three miles limit.
b) coastal waters, including any waters up to the limit of the highest tide; or the fresh-water limit of river or watercourse.
c) inland freshwaters, includes lake or pond relevant river or watercourse above the fresh-water limit.
d) ground waters…any waters contained in underground strata.

Section 104 (2) provides that the waters of any lake or pond or of any river or watercourse include a reference to the bottom, channel or bed of any lake, pond, river or, as the case may be, watercourse which is, for the time being, dry.

The Environment Agency has to keep a public register of information relating to the regulation of controlled waters under s.190 WRA 1991, including discharge consents.

Abstraction of water

The Environment Agency regulates the abstraction of water through the WRA 1991. Water Resources (EIA) Regulations 2003, require an EIA to be carried out for projects which involve the abstraction of water (*e.g.* agriculture including irrigation) and which the Environment Agency considers will have a significant effect on the environment.

Consents to dispose of trade effluent into sewers

Sewerage undertakers are able to grant trade effluent consents for disposal of effluent into their sewers under s.188 of the WIA 1991. The sewerage undertaker then requires a discharge consent from the Environment Agency under WRA 1991 to discharge the treated effluent into controlled waters. Section 87 of the WRA 1991 provides a defence to an offence committed under s.85 of the WRA 1991, if a sewerage undertaker fails to treat unlicensed effluent it has received, see *NRA v Yorkshire Water Services* (1995).

Consents to discharge into Controlled waters

The discharge consent system, contained in Sch.10 to the WRA 1991 (as amended), is the method by which the quality of the water environment is controlled. An operator has to apply to obtain a discharge consent from the regulator, the Environment Agency, before being able to make any discharges of trade or sewage effluent into controlled waters or out to sea. It is not necessary to obtain a discharge consent, if permission has already been authorised by another licensing system, *e.g.* IPC authorisation, IPPC permit. The Environment Agency has powers to review, revoke and vary the conditions of a discharge consent and there is a right of appeal to the Secretary of State.

If water pollution comes from a process with a permit under IPPC, then the Environment Agency will take action under PPCA Act 1999. PPCA 1999 enables the Environment Agency to check the processes that have caused the pollution and if necessary amend the conditions of the permit. It is a defence to an offence under s.85 of the WRA 1991, to have discharged in accordance with a discharge consent. Under s.86 of the WRA 1991, the Environment Agency can serve a Prohibition Notice on a person discharging into controlled waters, who does not require a discharge consent. The Prohibition Notice can either prohibit the discharge or impose conditions.

Principal offences to pollute controlled waters

The main offences to pollute controlled waters are under WRA 1991:

- s.85 offences of pollution controlled waters.
- s.86 applies to an offence committed under s.85, where the person is contravening a Prohibition Notice.
- s.87 applies in respect of offences under s.85 where the discharges are into or from public sewers.

Prosecution can also be taken under s.4(1) Salmon and Freshwater Fisheries Act 1975, if a person puts into any waters containing fish or their tributaries, any liquid or solid matter which makes the waters poisonous or injurious to fish or their spawning grounds. Under s.217 of the WPA 1991, Company Directors and other senior managers can be held liable personally for actions of their employees, in addition to offences committed by the Company In *NRA v Alfred McAlpine Homes East Ltd* (1994), the Company was held vicariously liable for the acts of its employees.

Under s.85 (1) of the WRA 1991 it is a strict liability offence if 'A person contravenes this section if he **causes** or **knowingly** permits any poisonous, noxious or polluting matter or any solid waste to enter any controlled waters'. Prosecution under s.85(1) has often depended on interpretation of words in the section, in particular 'cause' or 'knowingly permitted'. In *R v Dovermoss Ltd* (1995), the Court of Appeal held that 'polluting matter' meant 'matter' that was capable of causing harm.

To 'Cause' or 'knowingly permitted'

A number of prosecutions under s.85 (1) have concerned whether the defendant's actions could be deemed to have caused or knowingly permitted the pollution. The appellants in *Alphacell v Woodward* (1972) were paper manufacturers who had a plant on a river bank. Overgrowth of leaves, etc. got into their pump system, causing it to fail and polluting effluent entered the river. The appellants were convicted of 'causing' polluted matter to enter the river contrary to s.2(1) of the Rivers (Prevention of Pollution)

Act 1951. They appealed on the grounds that 'knowingly' should be implied to mean 'causes'. The House of Lords dismissed the appeal and defined 'causes'. A person could cause a result if he is negligent, without intending the result. Lord Wilberforce stated that causing 'must involve some active operation or chain of operations involving, as a result, the pollution of the streams'.

Wychavon DC v NRA (1993) concerned the escape of sewage from a sewer under control of the LA, acting as an agent of the water authority, in maintaining a sewerage system. Cause of the sewage leak was due to a blockage. The Divisional Court held that, although the LA had remained inactive, it was not liable. In *Wrothwell v Yorkshire Water Authority* (1984), a company director poured a herbicide into a drain he thought led to a public sewer, but which led to a local stream. The Court of Appeal found him guilty of causing the water pollution, even though it was unintended, as it was a strict liability offence.

A factory pipe fractured, allowing cleaning fluid to escape into a storm drain and then controlled waters, *CPC (UK) Ltd v NRA* (1995). The fracture was caused by defective work carried out by subcontractors for the previous owner. The current owner had a rigorous environmental audit of premises before purchase, but had failed to detect the defective pipe. The conviction against the factory was upheld; they caused the pollution as they were operating the factory at the time of the incident.

In *Price v Cromack* (1975), a farmer had a contract with a firm to discharge waste into his lagoon, the lagoon wall collapsed and the waste escaped, severely polluting the river. The farmer was found not guilty of causing pollution as he had permitted the accumulation and not caused the resulting pollution. In *NRA v Yorkshire Water Services* (1995), an industrial solvent was illegally discharged into the sewer by an unidentified firm. The solvent went through the sewage works and, due to the design of the works, was able to enter controlled waters in an undiluted form. The House of Lords held that the sewerage undertaker had caused the pollution, although the conviction was quashed under a defence in s.87(2).

In *Att-Gen's Reference (No.1 of 1994) (CA Criminal Division)* (1995), the sewage undertaker was held to have caused water pollution by running sewage system in unmaintained state. It was argued that this was an omission (the undertaker failed to maintain the system, which is being inactive). The Court reformulated the issue by stating the active system was running sewage system in an unmaintained state. The Court also stated that it was possible for more than one person to be liable for causing a pollution incident.

Intervening Events

The chain of causation can be broken by an intervening act. Fuel oil from a tank was released into River Severn, causing pollution. The Company successfully plead that this was caused by a trespasser, in *Impress (Worcester) Ltd v Rees* (1971). In *Southern Water Authority v Pegrum* (1989), heavy rain filled slurry lagoons, which overflowed and polluted a river. It was held that this was not so out of the ordinary as to break the chain of causation (as in *Alphacell*, an accumulation of leaves are expected in the autumn). Oil from company storage tanks leaked into controlled waters after the tank was interfered with by vandals in *NRA v Wright Engineering CoLtd* (1994). It was held that the company was not responsible for the pollution, but the issue of the foreseeability of the vandalism was a factor in deciding liability.

A stricter approach was adopted in *Empress Car Co (Abertillery) Ltd v National Rivers Authority* (1998) which also concerned oil polluting a river. The oil had come from a tank, tampered with by vandals and had caused pollution via a storm drain. The oil was not retained by the protective bund as the company had set up a system to discharge oil outside the bund. The House of Lords held that the company were guilty of causing pollution. They had 'done something', *i.e.* maintained a diesel tank', although not this need not be the immediate act that led to the pollution. Lord Hoffman reaffirmed *Alphacell* rules on causation, '*The true common sense distinction is . . . between acts and events which although necessarily foreseeable in the particular case, are in generality a normal and familiar fact of life, and acts or events which are abnormal and extraordinary*'.

Some circumstances might be very unexpected, it is up to the courts to decide. In *Express Ltd v Environment Agency* (2003), a milk tanker had a burst tyre on the motorway. The tanker delivery pipe had been severed and large quantity of milk escaped, the driver pulled over to the hard shoulder, where the rest of the milk was discharged into 2 storm drains that ran into a brook. The defendant was found guilty under s.81 of the WRA 1991, but appealed by way of case stated to the High Court, on the grounds that; 1) the sequence of events broke the chain of causation; and 2) the defence of s.89(1) applied as the milk was discharged in an emergency so as to avoid danger to life or health. The Court stated that 'extraordinary events' referred to in the *Empress Car* Case, meant an intervention by a 3rd party or a natural act. However, the court allowed the appeal on the 2nd grounds, the defence of s.89(1) as the actions to pull off the road, near to the drains, could be considered to have been done in an emergency to avoid danger to life or health.

Defences to s.85–7 of the WRA 1991

Section 88 of the WRA 1981 provides a defence to principal offences in respect of authorised discharges under the various licences, IPC authorisation, IPPC permit, waste management licence, etc. Section 89 provides defences in principal offences, including s.89(1), where the pollution is caused in an emergency, to avoid danger to life or health., see *Express* milk tanker Case. In *Taylor Woodrow Property Management v NRA* (1995), a property company held a discharge consent relating to an outfall from an industrial estate. There was a discharge which contravened the consent and even though the property company did not personally cause the discharge, as holders of the consent, they were prosecuted. A latent fault in a pipe was considered to be ordinarily expectable and the owner was held responsible for the escapes through the broken seal even though he had no knowledge, *Environment Agency v Brock Plc* (1998).

Section 87 provides defence for sewerage undertakers. It is not a defence to have failed to treat effluent that the sewerage undertaker is licensed to accept, but it is a defence to have failed to treat unlicensed effluent it has received.

Penalties

On conviction of a water pollution offence under WRA 1991, the penalty on summary conviction is a fine up to £20,000 and/or imprisonment for up to 3 months. On indictment, the penalty is an unlimited fine and/or imprisonment for up to 2 years. Milford Haven Port Authority was prosecuted under s.85 of the WRA 1991, following the Sea Empress oil tanker disaster. The Port Authority was fined £4 million pounds, later reduced to £75,000 on appeal, *Environment Agency v Milford Haven Port Authority (Sea Empress)* (2000).

Action by individuals

Some Acts state that only the regulator can take a prosecution, but s.100 of the WRA 1991 protects individuals rights to take criminal action. Greenpeace took an unsuccessful private prosecution under WRA 1991 in *Greenpeace v ICI* (1994). Individuals can also take a judicial review to challenge the actions of public bodies, such as the regulator or a statutory sewerage undertaker. In *R. v Secretary of State for ETR Ex p. Standley* (1997) the applicant used judicial review to challenge whether the Nitrates Directive have been correctly transposed into UK law. The court referred the case to ECJ for a preliminary ruling.

Prevention of Pollution

Under s.161A of the WRA 1991, the Environment Agency has the discretion to prevent the pollution of controlled waters by issuing an anti-pollution works notice where any poisonous, noxious or polluting matter or any solid waste matter is likely to enter controlled waters. The Notice is served on the person who causes or knowingly permits the matter to be present in controlled waters, or present in a place where it is likely to enter controlled waters. It is an offence to fail to comply with the notice. The Environment Agency can carry out the work in situations where the works needs to be carried out without delay, or no person can be found to serve the Notice on, and recover expenses. Following civil action in the *Cambridge Water Company Case* (1994), the Environment Agency later pursued ECL Plc for remediation of the land under s.161A of the WRA 1991.

Section 92–5 of the WRA 1991, provides the Environment Agency with powers to introduce measures to prevent pollution, including the setting up of Water Protection Zones and Nitrate Sensitive areas. The Environment Agency issue advice on best operational practices and also Pollution Prevention Guidance Notes.

OTHER STATUTORY CONTROLS

IPC/PPC regime

Under EPA 1990, the Environment Agency regulates emissions to land, water and air by industrial processes through the IPC regime. IPC is being replaced by the PPC regime introduced by the PPCA 1999. PPC regime includes IPPC processes which produce emissions into the air, water or land. The Environment Agency will regulate the potentially more polluting processes under Part A1 Installations. The LA will cover emissions from the lesser polluting processes under Part A2 installations (also known as LA-IPPC), although the Environment Agency will act in a supervisory role in respect of water. As some IPPC permits will include discharges into sewers, they will be some overlap with the water regime .

Waste Management Licence

Under Reg.15 of the Waste Management Licensing Regulations 1994, before a waste management licence can be issued, the regulator and the Environment Agency, must be satisfied that measures have been taken to prevent pollution of groundwaters.

Contaminated land Regime Part IIA EPA 1990

Section 78A (2) of the EPA 1990 covers the criteria for designating land as contaminated land. Land which causes, or is likely to cause, the *'pollution of controlled waters'* should be designated as contaminated. As even a trivial amount of pollution triggers the requirement to designate the land under s.78A, a clause is being added to the new Water Bill to amend s.78A(2) to *'significant pollution of controlled waters'*. A Remediation Notice under the contaminated Land regime, introduced in 2000, takes priority over an anti-pollution works notice under s.161 of the WRA 1991.

COMMON LAW—CRIMINAL ACTION

In 1988 South West Water Company polluted the drinking water supply and caused health problems for many local people in Camelford, Cornwall. In 1991 the water company were successfully prosecuted for public nuisance. If anyone died as a result of water pollution the polluter could face manslaughter/corporate manslaughter charges if the pollution was caused by gross negligence.

CIVIL ACTION

Section 100 of the WRA 1991 specifically provides that no civil rights of action are conferred in respect of offences, nor does it withdraw any rights to remedies (either civil or criminal) in respect of Part III of the Act (ss.82–104). Under s.100(B) of the WRA 1991, compliance with a discharge consent does not provide a defence in civil action. Riparian rights are those rights enjoyed by owners of land adjoining a river. As well as riparian owners wishing to enforce their rights, others who have suffered from water pollution may seek to take civil action under tort.

Torts

Depending on the circumstances, a claimant might have a claim in one or more of the following torts: negligence, nuisance, *R. v F* or trespass.

A brewery successfully sued in **nuisance** when its well was contaminated by sewage from a neighbouring well, *Ballard v Tomlinson* (1885). *Cambridge Water Co v Eastern Counties Leather Co* (1994), the plaintiff unsuccessfully tried to make a claim in **negligence, nuisance** and *R. v F* in respect of pollution to its water supply caused by contamination from neighbouring land. The House of Lords held that foreseeability of harm of the relevant type by the defendant was a prerequisite of the recovery of damages both in nuisance and under the rule in *R. v F.* In *Savage v Fairclough* (1999), the Court of Appeal dismissed a claim in **nuisance** in respect of spring water contaminated by nitrates as the defendant had used good farming practice at the relevant time. In *Marcic v Thames Water* (2002), the sewerage undertaker failed to remedy flooding caused by their sewer system onto the property of Marcic. The Court of Appeal held that the High Court had been correct to conclude that Thames Water had infringed the claimants rights under Art.1 of the first protocol of Human Rights Act 1998 Act, but any right that the claimant had to damages under that Act was, however, displaced by his common law right to damages under **nuisance**.

One of the advantages of taking action in **trespass** is that it is not necessary to show harm has been suffered. In *Jones v Llanrwst Urban District Council* (1911), the owner succeeded in his claim in **trespass** in respect of sewage deposited on the plaintiff's land having travelled downstream. In *British Waterways Board v Severn Trent Water Ltd* (2001), a statutory sewerage undertaker discharging water into a canal without consent was considered **trespass**. In *Scott-Whitehead v National Coal Board* (1985), the plaintiff used water he abstracted from a stream under licence, to irrigate his crops. The water contained chlorine which damaged the crops and the plaintiff was awarded damages for **negligence** as the water company had failed to inform the plaintiff about the water quality.

The EU issued a draft directive for an environmental liability regime which may reduce the need to take action in tort.

---

11. ATMOSPHERIC POLLUTION

Atmospheric pollution has an adverse affect on both human health and the environment. Health problems include asthma, lung diseases, cardiovascular diseases and skin cancer. Apart from affecting localised air quality, atmospheric pollution can be trans-boundary and cause problems such as acid rain, global warming and depletion of the ozone layer. The Chernobyl disaster in 1986, where radioactive material was dispersed over nearly all of the northern hemisphere, illustrates how emissions into the air can cause wide-reaching harm to the environment and human health. Concerns over global issues has lead to a number of international treaties and UK laws have been shaped by both international and EU laws.

International Law

The UK has signed up to a number of international treaties, including:

- **1979 UN Convention on long range Trans-boundary Air Pollution** provides a framework for a number of protocols setting out emission levels for particular pollutants responsible for acid rain.
- **1985 UN Vienna Convention for the Protection of the Ozone Layer** and the subsequent 1987 Montreal Protocol, aims to reduce the main ozone deleting pollutants, including CFCs and halons.
- **1992 UN Convention on Climate Change** and subsequent 1997 Kyoto Protocol aims to reduce greenhouse gases. Countries are able to use various mechanisms to meet targets, including emissions trading systems, clean development mechanisms and carbon sinks.

European Union Policy

EU legislation in relation to air quality includes:

- **1984 Framework Directive on Emissions from Industrial Plant** with a number of 'daughter' directives.
- **1996 Framework Directive on Air Quality** with a number of 'daughter' directives for specific pollutants in the air.
- **1996 Integrated Pollution Prevention and Control Directive.**
- **2000 Waste Incineration Directive.**
- **2001 Revised Large Combustion Plant Directive** .
- **A number of Directives relating to product standards.**

Also **2000 Regulation on ozone depleting substances,** which takes direct effect and does not have to be transposed into national law.

STATUTORY CONTROLS

The main legislation to control air pollution is:

- Licensing of air emissions through: IPC/LAPC (Part I EPA 1990), being replaced by IPPC/ LAPPC (PPCA 1999).
- Clean Air Act 1993.
- Statutory nuisance s.79 of the EPA 1990.

Human Rights and Human Rights Act 1998

The actions of a public body have to be compatible with HRA 1998. A case heard by ECHR, *Lopez Ostra v Spain* (ECHR) (1995), concerned a family whose health had been affected by air pollution from a nearby waste plant which had been allowed to operate without a licence. ECHR held that Art.8 had been breached, and compensation was granted. ECHR case, *Guerra v Italy* (ECHR) (1998), concerned the failure of a public authority to give information to local residents about the risks of air pollution from a factory discharging gases into the environment. A claim under Art.2, Right to Life, was found inadmissible as the ECHR had already found Art.8 had been breached.

Town and Country Planning Act 1990

A planning application to build a superstore in Bath (a World Heritage Site) was refused by *Bath and North Somerset DC*, on grounds that air pollution was an issue of material consideration. However, the Planning Inspector was of the opinion that development would reduce traffic flow and allowed the appeal by *Safeway PLC* (1996). *R. v Bolton MBC Ex p. Kirkman* (1998), concerned an unsuccessful challenge to the LPA's decision to allow a waste recovery system, including failure of the LPA to consider the potentially damaging air emissions. The Court of Appeal held that the LPA was entitled to take account of the IPC regime unless the Environment Agency had indicated concerns about the emissions, which it had not done.

In *R. (Vetterlein) v Hampshire CC* (2001), the court held that the grant of planning permission did not engage their rights under Art.8 of the Act, as their concerns regarding the increase in air pollution levels from a proposed incinerator were only a general environmental concern. However, each case has to be decided on its merits and in other circumstances, rights under Art.8 could be engaged.

The existing IPC /LAPC regime

The IPC/LAPC regime under Part 1, EPA 1990, is being phased out by 2007. Under IPC, operators of the potentially most polluting processes require prior authorisation from the Environment Agency before certain prescribed substances can be discharged into the environment, including emissions into the air. The Local Air Pollution Control (LAPC) regime, enforced by LAs, deals the control of air emissions from less polluting substances.

The incoming PPC regime

Following the EC IPPC Directive, an integrated pollution prevention and control regime (PPC) was introduced by the PPCA 1999 and by 2007 will have completely replaced the IPC/LAPC regime. PPC requires industrial operators to obtain permits to operate certain listed processes, to ensure that the methods they use will prevent, reduce and eliminate pollution at source, including emissions into the air. PPC has 2 parts: IPPC which refers to part A1 and A2 installations and LAPPC which refers to Part B installations. Part A1 installations covers emissions to air, land and water of potentially more polluting processes and regulated by the Environment Agency. Part A2 Installations (also known as LA-IPPC) covers emissions to air, land and water of those processes with a lesser potential to pollute, and regulated by LAs. Part B installations covers the same installations as existing LAPC and regulated by the LAs.

Statutory Nuisance (EPA 1990)

Statutory Nuisance, ss. 79–82 of the EPA 1990, is regulated by the LA and applies to certain matters which are prejudicial to health or a nuisance. Emissions controlled by the IPC/LAPC, PPC regime and Clean Air Act 1993 are excluded from Statutory Nuisance, although this does not prevent an individual taking action to abate the nuisance under s.82. The following matters can apply to airborne pollution:

- Section 79(a), any premises in such a state so as to be prejudicial to health or a nuisance, (*e.g.* a damp property may affect air quality).
- Section 79(b), smoke, fumes or gases emitted from premises so as to be prejudicial to health or a nuisance, (excludes 'dark smoke' regulated by the CAA 1993).
- Section 79(c), any dust, steam, smell or other effluvia arising on industrial, trade or business premises.

Clean Air Act 1993 (CAA 1993).

Clean Air Acts of 1956 and 1968 and the Control of Smoke Pollution Act 1989 have been consolidated into Clean Air Act 1993. The Act does not apply to any processes regulated under the IPC/LAPC or PPC regime. Smoke emissions covered by CAA 1993, are excluded from Statutory Nuisance. The Act is regulated by the LA.

Offences under Clean Air Act 1993

Section 1 prohibits the emission of dark smoke from chimneys and furnaces. Section 1(1) applies to a chimney of any building and the occupier of the building is liable for any offence committed. An offence committed by a person in respect of a domestic premises is liable for a fine of up to the maximum of level 3 on the standard scale and for other premises, a fine up to level 5. Section 1(2) applies to furnaces which serve fixed boilers or industrial plants and the person in possession of the boiler or plant is liable for any offences committed. Section 2 prohibits the emission of dark smoke from industrial trade premises. Either the occupier of the premises or the person causing or permitting the emission is liable for the offence. A person found guilty is liable for a fine not exceeding £20,000

Section 5 limits the emissions from the chimneys of furnaces. Section 5(2) provides for the Secretary of State to prescribe limits on chimneys of furnaces and s.5(3) prohibits grit and dust to be emitted from a chimney at a rate exceeding the relevant limit. The occupier of any building in which the furnace is situated is liable for any offence committed. Section 5(4) provides for a defence of use of BPM for minimising the emission. On conviction, the defendant is liable to a fine not exceeding level 5 on the standard scale. Section 4 provides that furnace over a certain size require permission from LA before installation. Section 14 and s.15 regulate the height of chimneys. Section 20 prohibits smoke emissions in a smoke control area. Section 18 provides for LA (and s.19 in respect of the Secretary of State) to designate a Smoke Control Area which further restricts smoke emissions.

If an offence has been committed, the LA has to promptly inform the person responsible, with confirmation in writing within 4 days, failure to do so is grounds for a defence. These are strict liability offences, although there are some exemptions and defences.

National Air Quality Strategy (Environment Act 1995)

Part IV (s.80–91) of Environment Act 1995 (EA 1995) is designated to 'Air Quality' and contains provisions to implement Government policies from its 1995 Policy document, 'Meeting the Challenge' on air quality. Under s.80 the Secretary of State has a duty to publish an Air Quality Strategy and under s.80(4) is required to review the strategy from time to time. The Air Quality (England) Regulations 2000 (as amended) sets out air quality targets, to be phased in by 2008, in relation to key pollutants. Under s.87 EA 1995, the Secretary of State has a number of powers in relation to air quality, including implementing International and EU law obligations, national air quality strategy and air quality standards. Section 88 provides for the Secretary of State to issue guidance to LAs in connection with their duties under Part IV.

LAs are under a duty to review air quality from time to time under s.82 of the EA 1995 and identify areas where the air quality strategy is not being achieved and if so, under s.83, make an order to designate an Air Quality Management Area. If a subsequent review shows standards are being met, the order can be varied or revoked. Once an area has been designated an AQMA, under s.84 the LA have a duty to make an action plan to improve air quality.

Pesticide legislation

In 2003, DEFRA announced Government plans to introduce greater access to information concerning the notification and disclosure of crop spraying activities and introduce buffer zones between spraying areas and residential properties in England and Wales.

Miscellaneous legislation to control vehicle Emissions.

Vehicle emissions cause significant air pollution and various policies and subsequent legislation attempt to reduce polluting emissions and traffic levels. RCEP first highlighted the problems of air pollution from motor vehicles and increases traffic growth in its 1st report in 1971. In its 18th report, in 1994, RCEP made recommendations in relation to air quality targets and reduction of carbon emissions. A number of EU directives relating to emissions from motor vehicles have been transposed into UK law. Under s.14(2) of the Road Traffic Regulations Act 1984, the LA has power to restrict traffic flow or close roads if there is a 'likelihood of danger to the public'. In a judicial review, *R. v Greenwich LBC Ex p. W (a minor)* 1997, the Court of Appeal refused to make a declaration that pollution from road traffic was causing danger to the public and asthmatic children in particular, on the grounds that the Act only applied to danger caused by vehicles or pedestrians by way of accident, not danger to public health.

Other legislation

The Health and Safety at Work Act 1974 controls air pollution in the work place and is regulated by the Health and Safety Executive. Radioactive Substances Act 1993 regulates all aspects of radioactive materials, the keeping and using of radioactive materials and the accumulation and disposal of radioactive waste.

Common Law—criminal action

Air pollution could result in common law offences. The Court of Appeal upheld the decision to grant an injunction in public nuisance against a quarry whose operation had caused dust and vibration over a widespread area, *Att-Gen v PYA* (No.1) (1957). If a person died as a result of breathing air polluted by the actions of another, manslaughter/corporate manslaughter charges could be brought should the polluter had been grossly negligent.

Common law—civil action

An individual who suffers personal harm or loss due to air pollution caused by another, may be able to take action in tort.

Nuisance (private)

To sue in nuisance, the claimant has to suffer interference with the use of enjoyment and use of the land. In *Hunter v Canary Wharf Ltd* (1997), the House of Lords restricted damages, in respect of dust from building work, to those with a legal interest in the land. At an interim court hearing in respect of polluting emissions, in *McKenna v British Aluminium Ltd* (2002), the court stated there was an arguable case the restrictions of 'standing' in nuisance should be relaxed following Art.8 of the HRA 1998

Some farmers are expressing concern about risk of their crops being contaminated by GM crops. A farmer might have a claim in nuisance, if he could prove that the GM pollen drift had unlawfully interfered with his use and enjoyment of his land and he had suffered damage to his property (his crop) as a result. A court might award damages to a farmer if it could be shown that cross contamination resulted in him no longer being able to obtain a premium price for the crop having 'organic' or 'GM-free' status. It may become more difficult to sue in nuisance if domestic legislation is introduced to give rights to GM growers. In 2003 the European Commission issued a Commission Recommendation on guidelines for development of national strategies for the co-existence of GM crops with conventional and organic farming, which states *'that no form of agriculture be it conventional, organic or agriculture using GMOs, should be excluded from the European Union'*.

Rylands v Fletcher (R. v F)

A person could be liable in *R. v F* if he created fumes, dust, gases or other airborne pollution, which then escaped and harmed others. In *Hasley v Esso Petroleum Co Ltd* (1961) acid smuts escaped from the defendant's chimney which damaged the plaintiff's car, and emissions caused smells in the plaintiff's house. The claim succeeded even though the car was not standing on the land of the plaintiff and he was able to recover damages either on the basis of the doctrine of *R. v F* or public nuisance as he had suffered special damage. The plaintiff was also granted an injunction.

Negligence

A claimant may be able to take action in negligence, for harm or losses suffered due to air pollution, if the pollution occurred as a result of a breach of duty of care by the defendant.

Trespass

A claim might not succeed in trespass, unless direct interference can be shown. In the case of the spraying of pesticides or chemicals, the claimant will have to show that the defendant sprayed directly over or unto the claimant's land, rather than the spray be carried by the air currents. In circumstances where direct interference can not be proved, then a claim in nuisance or *R. v F* could be considered instead. In *McDonald v Associated Fuels Ltd* (1954), a successful claim in negligence, the court stated trespass would have also have succeeded on the facts. The plaintiff succeeded in a claim for trespass in *Kerr v Revelstoke Building Materials Ltd* (1976), because the crop duster had flown directly over their farm.

The EU has issued a draft directive for an environmental liability regime which may reduce the need to take action in tort.

12. NOISE POLLUTION

Noise generated by modern industrial processes, heavy machinery, cars, planes, building development, domestic products, loud music etc can cause significant noise problems for those living or working nearby. A substantial number of complaints that LA environmental health officers deal with each year are concerning noisy neighbours. Exposure to loud noise can result in health problems ranging from hearing loss to illnesses associated with sleep deprivation.

EU Policy

The EU has been responsible for a number of directives which reduce the noise emission from transport and products. The 2000 Noise Emission in the Environment by Equipment for Outdoors Directive has been transposed in domestic law by the 2001 Regulations. The 1996 IPPC Directive has brought noise and vibration into integrated pollution controls. The 2002 Assessment and Management of Environmental Noise Directive (Environmental Noise Directive) is due to be introduced into UK law in 2004. The aim of the Directive is avoid, prevent or reduce the harmful effects of exposure to 'environmental noise.' Environmental noise being unwanted or harmful outdoor sound created by human activities and the Directive will apply to road and rail infrastructure, aircraft outdoor and industrial equipment and mobile machinery

Government Policy

Most directives have been transposed into UK law by DEFRA, although ODPM is responsible for controlling noise emissions form aviation, vehicles and railways and DTI is responsible for noise emissions from outdoor machinery. DEFRA's Noise and Nuisance Policy, part of the Air and Environmental Quality Division, is responsible for developing initiatives to address noise and other statutory nuisance and manages research into noise issues. Its research projects include noise mapping in LA areas across the country and joint projects with the Department of Health on noise and health. DEFRA is developing strategies into ambient noise and neighbourhood noise (noise other than the workplace) and amendments to the Noise Act 1996. The Government is conducting a review of the Waste Permitting Regime.

Measurement of Noise

The control of Noise (Measurements and Registers) Regulations 1976 designates the use of decibels in measuring sound for statutory controls.

In *Hasley v Esso* (1961) the use of decibels to measure noise was confirmed and was defined as: 100–120 is deafening, 80–100 is very loud, 60–80 is loud and 40–60 is moderate noise.

STATUTORY CONTROLS

There are some acts which deal with specific work related noise. The main regulators of noise are LAs and the Environment Agency.

Human Rights Act 1998

HRA 1998 can be used to challenge the actions of the public bodies if they fail to protect the public from noise pollution; the relevant Articles being Art.8 and Art.1 of the First Protocol. Campaigners affected by noise from night flights at Heathrow Airport made an unsuccessful challenge in the domestic courts against the Government's decision to allow night flights. They then applied to ECHR, stating that the UK Government had violated their rights under Art.8 and Art.13. An interim judgment found in favour of the applicants in 2001, but in its final judgment, the ECHR held there had been no violation under Art.8 but that their rights had been violated under Art.13, the right to an effective remedy before national courts, *Hatton v UK Government* (ECHR) (2003). In a case heard in the English courts, *Dennis v MOD* (2003), the claimants succeeded in their nuisance action in respect of noise from RAF planes. However, the court stated that if their claim for nuisance did not apply, then their claim under Arts 8 and 1 of the first protocol would be relevant.

Town and Country Planning Act 1990

The planning system can reduce the risk of noise pollution at the time an application is made for building development or change of use of premises. Planning permission can be refused or include conditions which will reduce noise impact. For developments which require an EIA, any potential problems with noise pollution can be addressed at the planning stage. In *Gillingham BC v Medway(Chatham Docks Co)* (1993), if the problems of the port traffic using residential roads at night had been anticipated, restrictions could have been included in the conditions on the grant of planning permission.

Pollution Prevention and Control Act 1999 (PPCA 1999)

The PPC regime under the PPCA 1999 replaces the IPC regime, and brings noise and vibration under integrated pollution controls. Reg.2 of the Pollution Prevention and Control (E&W) Regulations 2000 defines the meaning of 'emission', which includes vibration, and provides that vibration and noise may be considered a 'pollutant' if harmful to human health or the quality of the environment.

Control of Pollution Act 1974

COPA 1974 Allows LAs to control the level of noise in their areas from construction works and applies to erection, construction, alteration, repair or maintenance of buildings, structures or roads, demolition and dredging works. Under s.60(2), the LA can serve a notice imposing requirements on the way work is carried out and it can be served as a preventative measure. When issuing a notice under s.60 the LA must consider: Codes of Practice under s.71 of the COPA 1974, the use of BPM to reduce noise and the affect of noise on the local residents. Contractors may choose to apply for a prior consent for noise emissions under s.61(3), giving information about the proposed works and how it is to be carried out. If the LA decides to grant consent, it may attach conditions. Section 62 provides the limited circumstances when loudspeakers can be used in the street. Under s.63, a LA can set up noise abatement zones, where it can monitor noise levels and issue a noise reduction notice if noise exceeds permitted levels.

Statutory Nuisance (s.79 of the EPA, 1990)

LA has a duty to serve an abatement notice on person responsible for causing a statutory nuisance, including noise. Section 79(1)(g) provides for noise emitted from premises so as to be prejudicial to health and s.79(1)(ga) provides for noise that is prejudicial to health or a nuisance and is emitted from or caused by a vehicle, machinery or equipment in the street. Section 79(1)(ga) was inserted into EPA 1990 by the NSNA 1993 to deal with noise from the street. Under s.79(7) 'street' means highway or any other road, footway, square or court, which, for the time being, is open to the pubic and 'noise' includes vibration. The 'person responsible' for noise from a vehicle includes the person who is registered owner of the vehicle and any other person who is the driver, s.79(7). The person responsible for noise from machinery or equipment, includes any person who is operating it, s.79(7).

The nature of noise nuisance is that it can be intermittent and the complainant may be advised to make a diary of the time and frequency of the noise and, if possible, details of other witnesses who can verify the nuisance. Once the LA is satisfied that a statutory nuisance exists, it must serve an abatement notice on the person responsible. If the LA fail to act, under s.82 an 'aggrieved person' can take action in the magistrates court.

There are a number of grounds of appeal, some specifically relating to noise. Defences to an abatement notice include 'reasonable excuse', the use of BPM (for industrial, trade and businesses) and a specific defence for noise. Under s.80(9), it is a defence to proceedings under s.80(4), if the noise was authorised under s.60 or s.61 of the COPA 1974. Section 81(6) provides a defence to s.81(5), if the noise was authorised under s.60 or s.61 of the COPA 1974. Under Reg.2(f)(ii) of the Statutory Nuisance Regulations 1995, it is grounds for appeal that the requirements of the abatement notice are more onerous than other notices in force, under COPA 1974 or NSNA 1993, in relation to the same noise.

LA powers to abate a nuisance under s.81(3) also include power to seize and remove equipment which is causing noise nuisance, as extended by s.10(7) of the NA 1996.

Noise Act 1996 (NA 1996)

The Noise Act, 1996 was introduced after a review was made into the effectiveness of Statutory Nuisance (s.79 of the EPA 1990) to deal with neighbourhood noise at night. Section 1 of the NA ,1996 gives LAs discretionary powers to enact additional noise laws. If they do so, under s.2 they have a duty to respond to certain complaints relating to noise, during 'night hours' between 11pm – 7am.

Investigating complaint during night hours

If a person, present in a dwelling, complains during night hours that excessive noise is being made from another dwelling, the LA have a duty to investigate the complaint. Under s.3 if the officer of the LA is satisfied that noise exceeding levels permitted is being emitted from a dwelling during night hours, he may serve a warning notice on the person responsible for the noise. The warning notice will state that if the noise exceeds permitted levels in specific period of time, the person may be guilty of an offence. The time period begins at a time specified by the officer, which must be a minimum of 10 minutes after notice issued, and until 7am. The person held responsible for the noise, is that person whose act, default or sufferance, or the emission of the noise is wholly or partly attributable. If the person responsible can not be found, the notice can be deemed served, by leaving it at the offending dwelling.

Penalties for non compliance with warning notice

If the warning notice is not complied with, an offence has been committed under s.4 and the person served with the notice is liable for a fine of up to level 3 on the standard scale (£1000). A defence of 'reasonable excuse' is available for this offence. Under s.8, the LA officer can issue a fixed penalty notice of £100 fine, which if paid within 14 days, will discharge the liability for conviction for the offence. Section 10 also allows the LA powers of entry and seizure to confiscate the noise making equipment; obstructing confiscation of the equipment also carries a fine.

Noise and Statutory Nuisance Act 1993

The LA have powers to deal with burglar alarms under s.9 of the NSNA 1993. When an alarm is installed, details of the key holder has to be registered with the Police. If an alarm has been activated for over an hour and is giving reasonable cause for annoyance, a LA officer has the powers to enter the building and switch it off. Section 8 of the NSNA 1993 amended s.62 of the COPA 1990 to allow use of loud speakers in the street in certain circumstances. It added s.79(1)(ga) of the EPA 1990, to provide for noise nuisance in the street.

Land Compensation Act 1973.

A LA has a duty to insulate buildings against noise created by public works such as road building. Residents living near Plymouth City Airport made a successful challenge that compensation was due under LCA 1973, in relation to building work, and this was upheld by the Court of Appeal. In *R. v Plymouth City Airport and Secretary of State for the Environment Ex p. Thomas* (2001).

Other Legislation

The Health and Safety at Work Act 1974 controls noise at the work place. Civil Aviation Act 1982 controls the noise created by aircraft. Some LAs make local byelaws to control noise and anti-social behaviour taking place in the street or on LA property or land. Conditions can be attached to licences issued for public houses to reduce noise nuisance. Public entertainment licences, also play a role in regulating noise levels.

COMMON LAW—CRIMINAL ACTION

Public nuisance

In *Hasley v Esso* (1961), a private nuisance action in respect of noise, the judge held that it could also have been a case of public nuisance. The LA took an unsuccessful action in public nuisance relating to noise, in *Gillingham BC v Medway (Chatham Docks Co.)* (1993). The LA had granted planning permission for a port at an old naval dockyard site. After the port started operating, residents complained about the noise and vibration from the lorries. The LA brought an action to declare that the use of the residential roads at night was a public nuisance and sought an injunction to stop lorry movements at night. The court found that, apart from extreme circumstance, lawful use of the highway could not be a public nuisance. The court had to consider the area with the planning permission which could change the character of a neighbourhood and whereas a nuisance could have been actionable before planning permission, it might not be afterwards.

COMMON LAW—CIVIL ACTION

Nuisance (private)

(Private) nuisance is the most likely action in civil law to abate noise nuisance and also claim damages. For an action in nuisance, the defendant must have interfered with the use and enjoyment of the land of the other. The claimant must have a legal interest in the land (*e.g.* owner, tenant), however following the HRA 1998, the courts may develop the common law to extend *locus standi* in nuisance, see *McKenna v British Aluminium Ltd* (2002). In deciding whether a nuisance exists, the courts will consider duration and frequency of interference, locality, nature of the nuisance, sensitivity of the claimant, intent of the parties and use of BPM to reduce the nuisance.

In *Hollywood Silver Fox Farm v Emmett* (1936), as the noise was to annoy, it constituted a nuisance, whereas in other circumstances it may have been an ordinary use of a property. In *Murdoch v Glacier Metal Co Ltd* (1998), the Court of Appeal held that the trial judge had applied the right test in taking into account the standards of the average person and the character of the neighbourhood when deciding whether the noise was sufficiently serious to amount to a nuisance. A LA tenant failed in her claim of (private) nuisance against the LA for inadequate soundproofing of flats, as the House of Lords held that the plaintiffs neighbours were using their properties in a normal way, *Baxter v Camden LBC (No.2)* (1999). *Dennis v Ministry of Defence* (2003), a nuisance action against the MOD due to the noise of the military aircraft flying overhead. The judge did not order the nuisance to stop but awarded nearly £1 million in damages for loss of amenity, loss of business opportunities and loss of value of the property, an historical country estate.

Other Torts

In *Hunter v Canary Wharf Ltd* (1997), a claim in connection with dust and noise, initially included a claim under *Rylands v Fletcher*, although this was later abandoned. In circumstances where excessive noise has caused harm or loss, and the claimant does not have standing in nuisance, there may be grounds for a claim in negligence.

Contract law

In *Farley v Skinner* (2001), the House of Lords awarded a home buyer damages against a surveyor for breach of contract after negligently reporting that the property would not be affected by aircraft noise from Gatwick. Land owners may place restrictive covenants on the land to prevent future occupiers/owners carrying out certain activities likely to cause nuisance or excessive noise.

Mediation

The public are increasingly encouraged to use mediation as a way of resolving disputes for such issues as noise problems.

13. WASTE MANAGEMENT

Background

Waste is the discarded by-products of processes or products and, along with other industrialised societies, the UK produces a high level of waste. Nowadays, the main methods of waste disposal are deposit in a landfill site or incineration, both of which have drawbacks. Incinerators cause air pollution, high cost of building the incinerator and disposal of residues following incineration. Historically, waste was buried in rubbish dumps, this has increasingly become a problem with both the large amount of volume of waste produced and the difficulties associated with burying mixed waste. Buried waste matter can break down and contaminate neighbouring land, produce toxic gases or cause groundwater pollution. In response to concerns about waste in the early 1970's, the Government produced 2 reports on waste disposal, which resulted in the Control of Pollution Act 1974 (COPA 1974). COPA 1974 introduced a waste disposal licensing system for the disposal of 'controlled waste'. The Deposit of Poisonous Waste Act 1972 (now repealed) was introduced, making it an offence for any poisonous, noxious or polluting waste to be deposited on land in a way likely to create an environmental hazard.

In 1990, the Government published a white paper 'This Common Inheritance' in respect of its polices for environmental pollution. Its waste policies included giving priority to waste minimisation, recycling waste and targets for recycling waste by LAs, with the emphasis moving from control of waste disposal to waste management. Part II of the Environmental Protection Act 1990 (EPA 1990) replaced Part I of the COPA 1974, introducing stricter licensing controls. Following the 1991 EU Waste Framework Directive, waste management licences covered storage, treatment and recycling of waste and were introduced in domestic law through the Waste Management Licensing Regulations 1994. Much of UK waste law is now derived from EU law, not only in relation to waste management licensing regime but also waste reduction and recycling initiatives.

International law

The 1989 UN Basel Convention on the Control of Transboundary Movements of Hazardous Wastes and their Disposal was introduced to stop the practice of industrialised countries sending their hazardous waste to developing countries for cheaper disposal. The Convention aims first, to minimise the generation of hazardous wastes, secondly, to dispose of hazardous wastes as close to source of generation as possible and thirdly, to reduce the movement of hazardouse wastes. Hazardous waste includes toxic, poisonous, explosive, corrosive, flammable, ecotoxic and infectious waste. The EC signed up to the convention and required all member states to ratify the Conventions. The UK introduced the Transfrontier Shipment of Waste Regulations 1994 to comply with the 1994 Council Regulation (EEC) No. 259/93 and the Waste Framework Directive in relation to imports and Exports. The only industrialised country which has not ratified the Basel Convention is the USA. In 1994, convention parties agreed to ban the export of hazardous waste from OECD to non-OECD countries (The Base Ban agreement)

EU Policy

The EU's Waste strategies are contained in the 5th Action Programme and Community Waste Strategy. The aims include: reducing waste at source, re-use or recycle of waste, use of waste as a source of energy and that waste should be disposed of in the country it originates from. Policies also put more responsibility on the recycling or recovery of waste products by the original producer.

The Main EU legislation being:

- Waste Oil Directive 1975.
- Groundwater Directive 1980.
- Waste Framework Directive 1975.
- Waste Framework Amendment Directive 1991.
- Hazardous Waste Directive 1991.
- Integrated Pollution and Prevention Control Directive 1996.
- Landfill Directive 1999 (includes tyres).
- Waste Incineration Directive 2000.
- Batteries and Accumulators Containing Certain Dangerous Substances Directive 1991 (with later updates).
- Packaging and Packaging Waste Directive 1994.
- End-of-Life Vehicles Directive 2000.
- Waste Electrical and Electronic Equipment (WEEE) Directive 2002 and Restriction of the Use of Certain Hazardous Substances in Electrical and Electronic Equipment (ROHS) Directive 2002.
- EC Regulation (2037/2000) to reduce the release of man-made CFCs and related compounds that cause damage to the ozone layer.

Current Government Policy

England and Wales produce 400 million tonnes of waste each year, of which 25 per cent is made up of household, commercial and industrial waste. About 35 per cent of industrial and commercial waste and 12 per cent of household waste is recycled or composted and the remainder goes to landfill sites. In the national sustainable waste strategy: 'Waste Strategy 2000', the Government sets out its aims to reduce, and where possible to re-use waste, to reduce the use of raw materials and the amount of waste needing disposal and increase the amount of household waste recycled or composted from 12 per cent to 25 per cent by 2005/6. In 2002, the Goverment Strategy Unit produced a report called 'Waste Not, Want Not (2002)' which highlighted the economic and environmental benefits of acting now to reduce waste volume and setting out measures to do so, including fiscal measures.

What is waste ?

There are various definitions of waste. The 1991 Waste Framework Directive (which amended the 1975 Directive) introduced a new definition of waste and the list of categories of substances or objects which could be considered waste are listed in Annex 1. The Directive was transposed into domestic law by Waste Management Licensing Regulations 1994 (WML Reg.1994) and Sch.4 amended s.75 of the EPA 1990. 'Waste' is now defined in s.75 of the EPA 1990 as 'any substance or objects in the categories set up in Sch.2B to this Act which the holder discards or intends or is required to discard *'being broken, worn out, contaminated or otherwise spoiled'*. Sch.2B (which is the same as Annex 1 of Waste Framework Directive), lists 16 categories of substances or objects which are considered waste provided they are discarded, including a final category of *'any materials, substances or products which are not contained in the above categories'*.

The Deparment of Environment Circular 11/94 gave advice on whether material is to considered waste. Materials will not be considered waste if sent to a recovery operation, but will be waste if sent to a disposal operation. Definitions of disposal and recovery operations are included in WML Regulations 1994.

Where UK law refers to 'Controlled waste' (meaning waste controlled by legislation), it now has the same meaning as 'Directive Waste' within the scope of the 1975 Waste Framework Directive (as amended). Controlled Waste includes Household, Industrial and Commercial waste. 'Controlled Waste' is either Inert, Non-Hazardous (non special) or Hazardous (special). More hazardous waste is defined as 'special waste' and has stricter controls on movement and disposal. Non-controlled waste which does not come under legislation, includes Agriculture and Mines/Quarries. Changes are being made to bring non-controlled waste under waste regulations.

Special Waste

Special Waste is defined under Special Waste Regulations 1996 (as amended). The 1996 Regulations were introduced to fulfil the UK's obligations under the EU 1991 Hazardous Waste Directive. 'Hazardous Waste' as defined in the Directive is included in the UK 'special waste' category. Household waste is excluded from Special Waste.

ECJ Cases regarding definition of waste

Palin Granit Case (2002) involves a case referred by Finland to the ECJ for a preliminary ruling as to whether a left-over stone from a quarry should be considered waste. The court held that although it was similar to the original raw material and posed no risk to health, it was essentially extraction residue and should be considered waste. *SITA EcoService Nederland BV* (2003) was referred by the Netherlands for a preliminary ruling as to whether a process could be considered a recovery under Annex 2B. The ECJ ruled that it must be possible for any waste treatment operation to be classified as either recovery or disposal and a single operation could not be classified as both simultaneously. In *Tombesi* (1998), the ECJ stated that in interpreting the 1975 Waste Framework Directive, attention should not be focused on 'discard' but on the recovery operations listed in Annex 2B. A preliminary ruling in *Inter – Environment Wallonie v Regione Wallonie* (1998) ruled that even if the substance had a commercial value or could be used directly or indirectly in a industrial process, it did not prevent it from being considered waste. The ECJ revised its definition when it gave a preliminary ruling in *ARCO Chemie Nederland Ltd* (2002). If a substance was treated by a methods of disposal or recovery as listed in Annex 2B` it was only one of the factors to be taken into account when considering whether the substance was waste. Two cases concerning the interpretion of 'recovery' in relation to incineration waste under the 1994 Packaging and Packaging Waste Directive were decided together by the ECJ in 2003. In *Commission v Luxembourg* (2003), waste incinerated in a municipal waste incinerator was considered disposal, not recovery, as the main aim was to burn the waste and not to replace other fuel for energy generation. In *Commission v Germany* (2003), waste sent to be burnt in a cement kiln, replacing another fuel, was recovery not disposal. This means that recovery of packaging material at dedicated municipal incinerators could not be included in member states' recycling targets under the 1994 Directive. The Commission is now considering whether the 1974 Waste Framework Directive should be amended. Another ECJ ruling in 2003 on the definition of waste was referred by the UK Government in respect of the *Mayer Parry Case*. The ECJ held that scrap metal cleaned and sorted ready for feedstock was not 'recycling', but it was 'recycled' when it had been reprocessed.

Domestic court cases regarding the definition of waste

In R. (*Castle Cement Ltd*) *v Environment Agency* (2001), the applicant sought a declaration that the Environment Agency had exceeded its powers by issuing notices under the 1994 Hazardous Waste Incineration Directive, on the grounds the fuel that the company had burnt (made from waste materials and used as an alternative to coal), was not hazardous waste under the 1975 Waste Framework Directive. The court held that the aim of the fuel manufacturer and the applicant was to 'discard' the fuel and it would undermine the effectiveness of the directive if the fuel was not categorised as waste, particularly bearing in mind its toxic nature.

Parkwood Landfill Ltd v Customs and Excise (2002), in a case regarding liability for landfill tax, the court held that material disposed of at a landfill site did not have to be useless to be considered waste, but the individual had to possess the intention to discard the material.

In *Mayer Party Recycling Ltd v Environment Agency* (1999), the claimant sought a declaration as to whether the scrap metal it handled constituted 'waste' under the WML Regulations. The high court found that materials to be re-used, rather than finally disposed of, and which did not require any recovery operation before re-use, were not to be considered waste. Materials which required a recovery operation before they could be re-used, were to be considered waste until the recovery operation had been completed. The court took into account the 2 ECJ cases, *Tombesi* (1998) and *Inter-Environnement Wallonie* (1998). In *R. (Mayer Parry Recycling Ltd) v Environment Agency (ref. to ECJ)* (2000), the Environment Agency and the Secretary of State sought a declaration that MPR Ltd was not entitled to packaging waste recovery notes. The case was adjourned, pending an application to the EJC for a definition of waste in relation to both 1975 Waste Framework Directive and Packaging and Packaging Waste Directive 1994. In 2003, the ECJ ruled on the preliminary matters regarding the interpretation of waste and stated that where the scrap metal was used to reproduce ingots, or sheets of coils of steel, it could be considered recycling but not where it was transformed into a secondary raw material by the sorting, cleaning and shredding of the scrap metal. The court also stated that 1994 Directive should prevail over the 1975 Waste Framework Directive in situations where it specifically regulated, but that the conclusion would have been reached if 'waste' and 'recycling' from the 1975 Directive had been considered.

In *Att-Gen's Ref (No.5 of 2000) Re, (CA(Criminal Division)* (2001), the Attorney General referred a point of law, regarding the definition of waste, to the Court of Appeal. His actions followed the acquittal in the criminal courts of a defendant charged with failing to properly dispose of controlled waste under s.34 of the EPA 1990, after the trial judge relied on the decision in the *Mayer Parry* case (1999). In the criminal proceedings, A-G submitted that the *Mayer Parry* case was inconsistent with the recent decisions of the ECJ (*ARCO Chemie Nederland Ltd* (2002) case) and with the Framework Waste Directive 1975. The Court of Appeal allowed the A-G's reference, holding that as the substance was capable of being discarded, it was capable of being classified as 'controlled waste'.

In the light of the ECJ rulings in 2003 on the *Mayer Parry* case and the 2 waste incineration cases, DEFRA is planning to issue further guidance on the definitions relating to waste. The definition of waste is a crucial issue; if a material is considered 'controlled (or directive) waste', it comes under waste legislation which is subject to criminal liability. There are implications for other waste directives as well, depending on where waste is incinerated, it may or may not count as recovery under 1994 Packaging and Packaging Waste Directive. The number of cases being referred to the ECJ courts, for a preliminary ruling in relation to the definition of waste, indicates the need for the ECJ to provide more specific guidance on the definition of waste.

The meaning of the word 'deposit' also affects waste law. In *R. v Metro. Stipendiary Magistrates Ex p. London WRA* (1993), it was held that 'deposits' included both temporary and permanent deposits. The court held that 'deposit' could be considered a continuing activity in *Thames Waste Management Ltd v Surrey CC* (1997) where it would be considered appropriate under the requirements of the WML Regulations.

STATUTORY CONTROLS

The main statutory controls are related to the waste management licensing regime and other legislation to reduce, recycle and recover waste. However, other laws impact on waste as well.

Challenging decisions and actions of public bodies

Lopez Ostra v Spain (ECHR)(1995), is a Spanish case, where the claimant took her case to the ECHR, claiming her family's human rights had been breached by air pollution from a nearby waste plant. It had been allowed to operate without a licence and the Government failed to act. The court held the family's rights had not been breached under Art.3, but they had been breached under Art.8 and compensation was granted.

R. (Vetterlein) v Hampshire CC (2001) involved an unsuccessful judicial review against a decision to allow planning permission for a waste incinerator on the grounds that the residents' human rights had been breached. The Court found that the claimants had a generalised concern as to the effects of the incinerator in terms of increased nitrogen dioxide emissions and such generalised environmental concerns did not engage Art.8 of the HRA 1998. The House of Lords held that Art.6(1) was concerned with the fairness of a trial and not with extra judicial inquiries, *R v Hertfordshire CC Ex p. Green Environmental Industries* (2000). The case concerned a local WRA who had found and disposed of a large quantity of clinical waste from the applicant's land. The applicant was not licensed to keep waste on the site and refused to supply information regarding the wasteas required under s.71 of the EPA 1990, without receiving confirmation that the information would not be used in a prosecution.

Town and Country Planning Act 1990 (TCPA 1990)

Minerals and Waste local plans are prepared by County and some unitary authorities and National Parks. Development plans also include policies relating to waste. All new development or change of use of land requires planning permission under TCPA 1990. A grant of planning permission of a landfill site might include a condition, *e.g.* limiting operational hours. If the development is likely to have a significant impact on the environment, an Environmental Impact Assessment is also required under Town and Country Planning (EIA) Regulations 1999. Under s.36(2) EPA 1990, before the Environment Agency can issue a waste management licence, the operator must have relevant planning permission or an established use certificate under the Town and Country Planning Act 1990.

The US "Ghost Fleet"

At the time of going to press, November 2003, there is legal controversy over a fleet of former US navy ships, dubbed the "ghost fleet", which were due to come to England for dismantling. Following legal challenges by environmentalists in the USA, only four of the fleet were allowed to be exported. The first 2 ships are now in dock having being towed across the Atlantic and a further 2 are on the way. Initially the Environment Agency granted a transfrontier shipment notification, under the Transfrontier Shipment of Waste Regulations 1994, to allow the ships to be brought into the country. The company applied to the Environment Agency for a modification of their waste management licence to enable them to increase their capacity, which was granted. When the company then applied to Hartlepool BC to renew planning permission granted over five years ago for a dry dock. The LPA informed the Company that an EIA would be required. The Company have since stated that work had already been started on the development of the dry dock and they intended to rely on the previous planning permission. The Environment Agency later stated the modified waste management licence was invalid on grounds the company did not have current planning permission for the dry dock (necessary for the dismantling work) and the licence did not cover the scrapping of ships. The Environment Agency also stated that the transfrontier shipment notification was invalid.

In November 2003, the High Court considered two judicial reviews. One by FoE to quash the grant of modified waste management licence. The Environment Agency agreed not to contest the application, but it was contested by Able UK. The other judicial review was taken by local residents to challenge the decision of both Hartlepool BC and the Environment Agency to allow the ships be dismantled. The High Court allowed an injunction to prevent any work being carried out on the ships, other than for safety reasons, prior to the full hearings to be heard in December 2003. The latest position is that the Secretary of State for the Environment, Food and Rural Affairs has issued a statement stating that following discussions with the US Department of Trade, the first two ships would be allowed proceed to Hartlepool, for safe storage, prior to return to US (possibly not until after the winter). The Secretary of State also stated that, as the proposed shipment to Hartlepool for dismantling can not be completed consistent with International and Community (EU) law, the law requires the ships to be returned to the US.

The Planning (Hazardous Substances) Act 1990

PHSA 1990 requires any development which wishes to keep any hazardous substances on, over or under land to obtain the consent of the Hazardous Substances Authority (LPA) who will ensure that the substance is stored and used appropriately.

Statutory Nuisance under s.79 of the EPA 1990

Deposited waste could be a statutory nuisance under s.79 of the EPA 1990, if prejudicial to health or a nuisance:

- Section 79(1)A: *'Any premises in such a state. . .'*,
- Section 79(1)C: *'fumes or gases emitted from (private) premises . . .'*
- Section 79(1)D: *'any dust, steam, smell or other effluvia arising on industrial, trade or business premise. . .'*
- Section 79(1)E: *'any accumulation or deposit which is prejudicial to health or a nuisance'*.

Contaminated Land

Under s.78YB(3) of the EPA 1990, a contaminated land re-mediation notice will not be served in respect of land contaminated by illegally dumped waste, if it can be dealt with by Environment Agency under s.59 of the EPA 1990 (waste legislation).

Waste Regulation

Part II (s.29–78) of the EPA 1990 (as amended) provides strict controls to ensure waste handling, disposal and recovery operations do not harm the environment or human health. More detailed provisions of the licensing system are contained in the Waste Management Licensing Regulations 1994 which is transposed in national law in the EU 1991 Waste Framework Directive, which amended the 1975 Directive.

Waste Authorities

Section 30 of the EPA 1990 created 3 levels of waste authorities:

- **Waste Regulatory Authorities.** WRAs were amalgamated into the Environment Agency by Environment Act 1995.
- **Waste Disposal Authorities.** WDAs are normally county councils (or metropolitan districts). Duties include setting up private waste disposal companies, providing municipal waste stations, transfer stations and making disposal arrangements for waste collected by WCAs.
- **Waste Collection Authorities.** WCAs are normally district councils or London boroughs.

Application for Waste Management Licence

The Environment Agency is the regulator of waste management provisions under Part II of the EPA 1990 (as amended). There are two types of waste management licence: a site licence (authorising the deposit, recovery or disposal of controlled waste in or on land) or a mobile plant licence (authorising the recovery or disposal of controlled waste from mobile plant). An application is made to the Environment Agency who under s.36(3) must consider:

- Whether Planning permission is in force,
- Whether the applicant is a fit and proper person; and
- Whether to reject the application if necessary to prevent pollution to the environment .

Variation, revocation, suspension or surrender of Licence

Section 37 of the EPA 1990 provides for licenses to be varied and under s 38 licences can be revoked or suspended. Under s.39, a licence can not be surrendered until the Environment Agency is satisfied all risks of pollution have ceased.

Waste Brokers and Carriers

Waste brokers arrange for the movement or disposal of waste for others. Reg.20 of the WML Regulations 1994 requires a waste broker to register with the Environment Agency unless they already hold a waste management licence, other statutory consents, charitable or voluntary registered waste carriers and WDAs and WCAs. Waste carriers are registered to transport controlled waste and are registered through Controlled Waste (Registration of Carriers and Seizure of Vehicles) Regulations 1991.

Activities exempt from Waste Management Licence

Reg.17 and Sch.3 of the WML Regulations 1994 provide a range of activities which are exempt from waste licensing controls, although such activity does have to be registered. It is an offence, under Reg.18 to carry out exempt activity without it having been registered. Special Waste does not normally come under exempt activities.

Acitivities excluded from Waste Management License

- **The IPC Regime:** If recovery/disposal of controlled waste is an integral part of IPC process, it is exempt from a waste management licence under Reg.16(1)A of the 1994 Waste Management Regulations. Section 28(1) of the EPA 1990 prevents a condition being attached to an IPC authorisation to regulate the final disposal of controlled waste.
- **The PPC Regime:** includes waste avoidance or minimisation. Schedule 1 PPC regulations 2000 lists activities which are subject to PPC regulations, including the waste management industry. The larger landfill sites come under PPC regulations, whilst the smaller landfill sites remain under part II EPA 1990.
- **Discharge of liquid waste:** Liquid effluent is regulated by Water Resources Act 1991 and the Urban Waste Water Treatment Regulations 1994.
- **Deposit of waste at sea:** licensed under the Food and Environmental Protection Act 1985.
- **Radioactive waste:** except where provided by the Secretary of State, under s.78 of the EPA 1990, nothing in Part II applies to radioactive waste within the meaning of the Radioactive Waste Act 1960.

Public Registers: The Environment Agency has to maintain a register with details for waste licences. Information can be excluded on the grounds of affecting national security and an individual or business can apply to have certain confidential information withheld from the register.

Waste Offences

a) Prohibition of the unauthorised or harmful depositing, treatment or disposal of waste   Under s.33(1) of the EPA 1990

'a person shall not (a) deposit controlled waste, or knowingly cause or knowingly permit controlled waste to be deposited in or on any land unless a waste management licence authorising the deposit is in force and the deposit is in accordance with the licence;

(b)   treat, keep or dispose of controlled waste, or knowingly cause or knowingly permit controlled waste to be treated, kept or disposed of

(i)   in or on any land, or

(ii)   by means of any mobile plant, except under and in accordance with a waste management licence;

(c)   treat, keep or dispose of controlled waste in a manner likely to cause pollution of the environment or harm to human health'.

Domestic household waste is exempt under s.33(2) as waste *'treated, kept or disposed of within the curtilage of the dwelling by or with the permission of the occupier of the dwelling is exempt from controlled waste controls. '*

Offences under s.33 are of 'strict liability', that is the defendant does not have to be negligent to be found guilty. In *Shanks & McEwan (Teeside) Ltd v Environment Agency*(1997), the waste company was found guilty under s.33(1)A of the EPA 1990, when the site supervisor failed to complete a new waste disposal form when waste was allocated to different storage. The Company appealed to the High Court and by way of case stated against its conviction in the magistrates court but was dismissed on the grounds that the knowledge required of the company was that waste was deposited on the land generally and did not have to have specific knowledge of the offending deposit of waste.

b) Other Miscellaneous Waste Offences   Section 33(6) of the EPA 1990 makes it a strict liability offence for a person to contravene any condition of a waste management licence. It is an offence under s.44 of the EPA 1990 to make a false statement in a waste management licence application. Section 60 makes it an offence to interfere with a waste site and receptacle for waste without the consent of the relevant authority, contractor or other person. It is an offence under s.63(2) if a person deposits waste which is not controlled waste, but if it were it would come under special waste.

c) Duty of care etc. in relation to waste   Section 34 of the EPA 1990, together with s.34(5) of the Environmental Protection (Duty of Care) Regulations 1991 (as amended) imposes a 'Duty of Care' on those who produce or handle waste from the point of creation through to final disposal or reclamation (from cradle to the grave). Section 34(6) makes it an offence to fail to comply with the duty of care imposed by s.34 or the 1991 Regulations. Section 34(1) provides that *'who imports, produces, carries, keeps, treats or disposes of controlled waste or, as a broker, has control of such waste'*. The Duty of Care requires the person to prevent the escape of waste from his control or that of any other person, ensure there is no unauthorised or harmful deposit, treatment or disposal of waste, to ensure on transfer of the waste is only to an authorised person or to a person for authorised transport purposes and that a written description is of the waste is also transferred. That there is transferred such a written description of the waste as will enable other persons to avoid a contravention of that section and to comply with the duty under this subsection as respects the escape of waste. Section 34(2) provides that the duty does not apply to an occupier of domestic property in respect of household waste produced on the property. Under s.34(3), the following are authorised persons: WCA, holder of waste management licence or waste disposal licence, and a registered carrier of Controlled Waste.

Defences

Compliance with the conditions of a waste management licence will be a defence to offences under s.33(1)A and s.33(1)B of the EPA 1990, but not s.33(1)C. s.33(7) provides defences for a person charged under that section:

a) *'that he took all reasonable precautions and exercised all due diligence to avoid the commission of the offence'*,
b) *'that he acted under instructions from his employer and neither knew nor had reason to suppose that acts done by him constituted a contravention of s.33(1)'*, or
c) *'that the acts alleged to constitute the contravention were done in an emergency in order to avoid danger to human health'*.

The person has to prove he took all reasonably practicable steps in the circumstances to minimise pollution and inform the Environment Agency as so reasonably practicable afterwards.

Penalties

Section 33(8) of the EPA 1990 provides that a person who commits an offence under s.33 is liable for: a) on summary conviction, a prison sentence not exceeding 6 months or a fine not exceeding £20,000 or both; and b) on indictment, a prison sentence not exceeding 2 years or a fine or both. Section 33(9) deals specifically with offences in relation to special waste. The penalty on summary conviction is the same as s.33(8)a, but on indictment under s.33(9)B the penalty is a prison sentence not exceeding 5 years or a fine or both. Section 157 of the EPA 1990 provides for senior managers of a company to be personally liable for offences committed under the Act.

Civil Liability in respect breach of EPA 1990

Under s.73(6) a person has a statutory civil remedy in respect of damage caused to another person in respect of waste deposited in or on land contrary to s.33(1) or s.63(2) of the EPA 1990.

Landfill legislation

In 1996, the Government introduced a landfill tax, administered by HM Customs and Excise, to encourage waste reduction, re-use and recycling. A landfill tax credit scheme was brought in to allow landfill operators to support environmental projects by giving a tax credit for donations to environmental bodies.

The EU Landfill Directive (Council Directive 1999) was transposed into UK law by Landfill Regulations 2002. Existing landfills had to show they could comply with the Directive. The main criteria of Landfill Regulations includes

- stricter engineering standards and monitoring required.
- staff need to be technically competent to manage the site.
- Sufficient financial provision for the cost of maintenance and aftercare requirements of the site. A landfill permit may only be surrendered when landfill is no longer a potential risk.
- 3 categories of sites, according to the waste it receives: Hazardous, Non-hazardous or Inert.
- No more co-disposal of waste. Hazardous sites can continue co-disposal until 2004.

- Biodegradable waste to be increasingly diverted away from landfill.
- Certain hazardous and other wastes, including liquids, to be banned from landfills.
- Wastes to be treated prior to disposal in landfill.

To meet the requirements of the Landfill Directive, the Government plans to increasingly restrict the amount of biodegradable municipal waste (BMW) that local WDAs can send to landfill. This will be achieved by new legislation and the Waste and Emissions Trading (WET) Bill is currently going through Parliament. WDAs will be allocated an amount they can send to landfill each year. If a WDA does not use its entire allowance, it can be sold to another WDA, and similarly if a WDA exceeds its allowance, it can buy surplus allowance from other WDAs. Its targets are: by 2010 to reduce the amount of BMW to landfill to 75 per cent of the amount produced in 1995, to reduce to 50 per cent by 2013 and 35 per cent by 2020. Under the Landfill Directive, the disposal of whole tyres in landfill sites stopped in 2003 and shredded tyres to stop by 2006.

Other Waste legislation

The Producer Responsibility Obligations (Packaging Waste) Regulations 1997 was introduced following the Packaging and Packaging Waste Directive 1994 and places recovery and recycling obligations on businesses who handle packaging. The Packaging (essential Requirements) regulations 2003 replaces 1998 Regulations.

The EU 2000 Regulation to reduce the release of man-made CFCs and related compounds that cause damage to the ozone layer requires CFCs to be removed from fridges and similar equipment. Being a regulation it automatically comes into force and does not have to be transposed into UK law.

The EU is currently proposing to revise the directive on batteries, to recycle more types of batteries and place responsibility on the producer for recycling. The End-of-Life Vehicles Directive 2000 sets targets of recovery of minimum 80 per cent of ELV for recycling by January 2006 and minimum of 85 per cent by January 2015. The UK is late in finalising legislation in respect of the ELV directive and the European Commission has referred the UK to the EJC. The WEEE Directive 2002 sets targets for collection, recycling and recovery of electrical and electronic products and the ROHS Directive 2002 bans the use of certain hazardous substances in their manufacture. Both the WEEE and ROSH directives have to be implemented into the law of the member states by August 2004.

In domestic legislation, the Household Waste and Recycling Act 2003 inserted s.45A, s.45B and s.47A into the EPA 1990 and provides for doorstep waste recycling collection by waste collection authorities in England and Wales. At a time when nearly all waste legislation is derived from the EU, unusually this Act was introduced to Parliament through a private member's bill. The Act aims to provide doorstep recycling of at least 2 materials by 2010 and it will divert more household waste away from landfill.

Future Legislation

The EU Water Framework Directive 2000 requires all inland and coastal waters to achieve 'good status' by 2015. This Directive is likely to have some impact on waste management, as inadequate disposal of waste can cause polluting matter to leach into groundwaters. The Euopean Commission has issued a Communicaiton in respect of an Integrated Product Policy (IPP), to reduce the environmental impact of products at each stage of their life cycle.

COMMON LAW—CIVIL ACTION

Torts

An individual might have cause of action in tort (negligence, nuisance, *R. v F* or trespass) in respect of damages due to a deposit of waste. Unlike statutory civil remedy for some offences under s.33 of the EPA 1990, there is no statutory civil remedy for breach of 'Duty of Care' under s.34 of the EPA 1990. However, a person could take action under one of the torts. To succeed in an action in trespass, it is sufficient to show that the waste has been deposited on the land, it is not necessary to prove that any harm or damages have been suffered. In *Blackburn v ARC Ltd* (1998), the plaintiff was awarded damages in (private) nuisance in respect of diminution in the value of his property due to smells and litter from a nearby licensed landfill site. The court rejected his defence of statutory authority because he held a waste disposal licence and had planning permission, as the nuisance was not unavoidable.

The EU has issued a draft directive an environmental liability regime which might reduce the need to take action in tort.

---

14. CONTAMINATED LAND

Background to contaminated land

Contaminated land includes industrial, mining and waste disposal sites. Historically, landfills have taken insufficient precautions against the leaching or escape of gases and chemicals. It may not be obvious that land is contaminated until soil testing and/or investigations are made into its previous land and that of neighbouring land. Contaminated land can be a threat to human health or the environment and can delay the development of brownfield sites. Contaminated Land is often cleaned up when the land is to be re-developed and planning application made to LPA. Land that is not remediated voluntarily is now dealt with by the contaminated land regime.

Possible consequences of contaminated land

Contaminated land can result in:

- Risk to human health (*e.g.* Love Canal, USA 1978, Lekkerkerk, Holland 1979).
- Risk to property (buildings, crops or animals subject to property rights).
- Risk of water pollution (*e.g. Cambridge Water Co* Case).
- Risk to the environment including nature conservation areas.
- Risk of explosion/fire from build up of gases (*e.g.* Loscoe, Derby 1986)

What are the problems of contaminated land?

- Cost of remediation.
- Deciding what level of clean up required.
- Pollution of land does not disperse (unlike emissions into air).

- Methods of clean up involve removal of the earth.
- Cost and availability of insurance for historic pollution, to indemnify current owner in case pollution is found on site.
- Brownfield sites may need to be cleaned up before proposed use.

EU Policy

Some European Union policies have resulted in directives which have some effect on contaminated land, including the 1980 Groundwater Directive and 1996 IPPC Directive. The EU is proposing a directive on environmental liability with regard to the prevention and restoration of environmental damage which would include contaminated land.

Government Policy

Following a Government consultation paper 'Let the buyer be better informed' a register for potentially contaminated land was introduced in s.143 of the Environmental Protection Act 1990. Later it was repealed as 'blighted' land was not necessarily contaminated, whilst some heavily contaminated sites would not be listed. In 1994, the Government consultation paper, 'Paying for our Past', resulted in a policy document 'The Framework for Contaminated Land'. These policy aims were implemented in s.57 of the Environment Act 1995 which inserted Part IIA, 'Contaminated land' into the EPA 1990 and came into force in 2000. The legislation provides for the identification and remediation of contaminated land, to prevent risks to human health or the environment. The level of clean-up depends on the current use of the land. The polluter pays principle is applied so that if the polluter is available, he should pay for the cost of the clean up. The Government has number of funding schemes for the clean up of contaminated land. The Finance Act 2001 allows companies who have bought 'contaminated land', to claim tax relief for remediation costs.

STATUTORY CONTROLS

The main legislation is the contaminated land regime under Part IIA of the EPA 1990, with further detail contained in the Contaminated Land (England) Regulations 2000. However, other legislation may apply to contaminated land and other regulatory regimes may overlap with the contaminated land regime.

Town and Country Planning Act 1990

LPAs should take into account land contamination or the potential for contamination, when preparing development plans and deciding planning applications. LPAs can impose a condition on planning permission so that the site is remediated to the satisfaction of the LA. Guidance for LPAs is contained in Planning Policy Guidance notes (PPGs). In *Bellway Urban Renewal Southern v Gillespie* (2003), the Court of Appeal found that the Secretary of State had erred in his decision that an EIA was not needed for the redevelopment of an old gas works 'on grounds that planning permission could include a conditions to remediate any contaminated land.' The correct approach was to decide whether an EIA was needed and if so, proposed measures would be assessed in the context of the EIA procedures. Under s.215 of the TCPA 1990, the LPA can serve an 'amenity notice' on an owner, or occupier, where the condition of his land is having an adverse affect on the amenity in the LPA's area or an adjoining area. An amenity notice would be served in circumstances where the problem is not sufficient as to warrant action under Statutory Nuisance.

Miscellaneous legislation

Under the Building Regulations 1991, Sch.1, C2, it states that: *'precautions shall be taken to avoid danger to health and safety caused by substances found on or in the ground covered by the building.'* Other legislation may help to reduce the likelihood of land becoming contaminated, *e.g.* legislation controlling use of pesticides and The Control of Substances Hazardous to Health Act 2002.

Contaminated land regime and overlap with other regimes

a) Statutory Nuisance   Under s.79(1)A of the EPA 1990 (as amended), land in a 'contaminated state is excluded from Statutory Nuisance. S79(1)B defines 'Contaminated stated' as *'if, and only if, it is in such a condition, by reason of substances in, on or under the land, that (a) harm is being caused or there is a possibility of harm being caused; or (b) pollution of controlled waters is being, or is likely to be, caused'.* The contaminated land regime differs in so much as it defines 'contaminated' as ....*significant harm is being caused or significant possibility of such harm'*. The difference in definition means that land that is not in such a state as to be *'significant harm'* or a *'significant possibility of such harm'* as to come under the definition of 'Contaminated Land' Part IIA of the EPA 1990, may also be excluded from the provisions of Statutory Nuisance. If a person was suffering health problems associated with land in a contaminated state, not covered by Part IIA, it might be possible to take action under another category for Statutory Nuisance, *e.g.* s.79(1)A, 'premises in such a state', or s.79(1)E, 'an accumulation or deposit'.

b) IPC/PPC   If land is contaminated as a result of breaches of IPC authorisation/ PPC permit, the regulator can take action under s.27 of the EPA 1990, rather than the contaminated land regime, s.78YB(1). Land can still be designated as contaminated even if a Remediation Notice can not be served.

c) Water Resources Act 1991   The contaminated land regime, under Part IIA of the EPA 1990, covers the pollution of controlled waters where the source is land which has been designated as contaminated land. The Environment Agency has powers under s.161 of the Water Resources Act 1991 to prevent the pollution of controlled waters by issuing an anti-pollution works notice. A works notice can be issued at the discretion of the Environment Agency, however as it is a requirement to serve a Remediation Notice, the contaminated land regime takes priority.

d) Waste Management   Under s.78YB(2), where land is contaminated as result of activities covered by a waste management licence, remediation notice can not be served, as action can be taken by the regulator under Part II of the EPA 1990. Section 78YB(3) applies to situations where controlled waste is illegally deposited on land, a remediation notice can not be served as the Environment Agency has powers to take action under s.57.

e) Radioactively contaminated land   The Contaminated land regime excludes radioactively contaminated land under Section 78YC, although it does allow the Secretary of State to modify regulations in respect of water pollution, the Radioactive Substances Act 1993 and other Acts as the Secretary of State considers appropriate.

In *Merlin v British Nuclear Fuels Plc* (1990), it was held that the radioactive contamination was not sufficient to cause physical damage, a claim for economic loss was outside the terms of s.7 of the Nuclear Installations Act 1965 and claims that their children were at increased risk of cancer, did not count as physical injury. A less restrictive approach was taken in *Blue Circle Industries Plc v Ministry of Defence* (1998), where a claim was made for damages in respect of land contaminated by radioactive material. The Court of Appeal upheld an award of £5 million as BCI had not only suffered pure economic loss but there had been physical damage to the property which reduced its value.

The Contaminated land regime: Part IIA EPA 1990

Part IIA of the EPA 1990, (as amended by s.57 of the EA 1995), is the main legislation for contaminated land and is supplemented by the Contaminated Land (England) Regulations 2000. Government guidelines are issued in 2000 DETR Circular 'Contaminated Land: Implementation of Part IIA EPA 1990'. Part IIA provides that the regulator (the LA) has to identify any contaminated land in its area, establish who is responsible for the contamination and ensure that the land is remediated, with the person(s) responsible paying for the cost of the clean up.

What is Contaminated Land ?

Section 78A(2) defines Contaminated Land as land which is *'in such a condition, by means of substances in, on or under land, that: a)The contaminant to cause significant harm to that receptor; OR there is a significant possibility of such harm being caused by that contaminant or receptor; OR b) Pollution of controlled waters is being or likely to be caused.*

Contaminated land has to have a 'pollutant linkage' between pollutant, a pathway and target, without a pathway and receptor, it should not be identified as contaminated land and can be contaminated by different causes or a combination of different pollutants, so there can be more than one significant pollutant linkage (SPL).

A **pollutant linkage** requires:

- **Contaminant (Pollutant)**; AND
- **Relevant Receptor (Target)**. (See Table A DETR Circular: human beings, property (buildings, crops or animals

subject to property rights), sites protected by nature conservation laws); AND

- **Pathway** which either allows EITHER: a) The contaminant to cause significant harm to that receptor; OR there is a significant possibility of such harm being caused to the receptor; OR b) Pollution of controlled waters is being or likely to be caused.

Definition of Significant Harm and Significant Possibility of Significant Harm

Section 78A(4) of the EPA 1990 defines 'harm' as meaning 'harm to the health of living organisms or other interference with the ecological systems of which they form part and, in the case of man, includes harm to his property'. Annex 3, Chapter A DETR Circular on Contaminated Land: defines *'Significant Harm'* and the *'Significant Possibility of Significant Harm'*, and A.23 states the LA should regard as significant only harm which is both: (a) to a receptor of a type listed in Table A, and (b) within the description of harm specified for that type of receptor in that Table.

Section 78A(5) of the EPA 1990 provides what harm is to be regarded as *'significant'* and whether *'the possibility of significant harm being caused is significant'* shall be determined in accordance with this guidance.

A.27 of Annex 3 gives the guidance. The DETR Circular gives categories of significant harm in Table A and Table B gives categories of significant possibility of significant harm

How is contaminated land identified and designated

Section 78B provides that the LA is under duty to inspect their area from time to time for contaminated land. If there is a reasonable possibility that the land is contaminated, the LA has powers to carry out field inspections. When contaminated land is found, a designation notice is issued to involved parties.

Special sites

Under s.78C(8), land which is considered to be the most seriously contaminated or widespread, is designated a special site and the Environment Agency becomes the enforcing authority. Section 78Q allows the Environment Agency to adopt the remediation notice of a special site. The 2000 Regulations list special site categories which includes: land on which IPC/PPC sites processes carried on, MOD land, etc. and in respect of pollution of controlled waters, where contamination is breaching drinking water quality standards.

To whom must Designation notice be given

Section 78B(3) provides that the LA must give notice to:
- a) appropriate agency (LA can consult the Environment Agency as to whether it should be a special site).
- b) owner of land
- c) any person who appears to be in occupation of whole or part of land
- d) an appropriate person. The 'appropriate person' being the person(s) responsible for paying the cost of the remediation. (There can be more than one 'appropriate person' and costs can be apportioned).

Remediation and service of Remediation Notice

Once the land has been designated as contaminated, the land has to be cleaned up to a certain standard (depending on its current or proposed use). Section 78G and s.78 H dispense with the period of consultation, if there is a risk of serious harm or serious pollution of controlled waters. If not, there is a minimum 3 month period for the enforcing authority to consult with the person(s) responsible for the cost of the clean-up of the land, and reach a voluntary agreement over remediation. If an agreement is reached, a signed remediation statement, stating the agreed work and timescale, is placed on the Public Register, s.78H(7). However, if unable to reach agreement, the enforcing Authority has a duty to require the contaminated land to be remediated. Section 78E requires the enforcing authority to serve a remediation notice on each 'appropriate' person, specifying what the person is to do by way of remediation of the land.

Exemptions to serving a remediation notice under s78H(5):

- Nothing in the way of remediation can be specified in notice.
- A voluntary agreement is reached.
- The enforcing authority is the appropriate person, as it either owns the land or has caused the contamination.

- Other statutory powers can be used to the enforce remediation.
- The enforcing authority has to take action under s.78N.
- There would be hardship for one of the appropriate persons under s.78N(3)(e), notice can not be served on other appropriate persons.
- In respect to pollution of controlled waters, the 'appropriate persons' are owners or occupiers.
- No 'appropriate person' can be found after reasonable enquiries have been made.

Who is the appropriate person, responsible for remediation

Section 78F designates who is responsible for remediation:

- **Class A**—the polluter is responsible. Any person or any of the persons, who caused or knowingly permitted the substances or any of the substances by reason of which the contaminated land in question is such land to be in, on or under land is an appropriate person
- **Class B**—the owner/occupier is responsible if no polluter can be found by reasonable enquiry.

Chapter D, Annex 3 DETR Circular, provides guidance on who should be excluded as members of Class A or Class B liability groups and apportionment of liability. Where Land has been contaminated by substances which have directly or indirectly escaped from other land, under s.78K, the 'appropriate person' will be the person who caused the contamination. The Caveat Emptor (buyer beware) rule does not apply in buying contaminated land, if the polluter can be located. The polluter is not liable if the land has been designated as contaminated and purchaser has bought with full knowledge.

'Causing or knowingly permitted' is similar to the water pollution offences under s.85 of the WRA 1991. There is a rebuttable presumption that the pollution was 'caused' by the person who owned or occupied the land at the time the contamination occurred. The owner/ occupier would have to prove he was not responsible for the contamination. Once the owner/occupier has been informed that the land is contaminated, he would not be considered to 'knowingly permit', unless he had the ability to take steps to prevent or remove that presence and had a reasonable opportunity to do so (see DETR Circular).

Section 78L provides that the person who has been served the remediation notice can appeal within 21 days. Appeals are heard by the magistrates court. For Special sites, the Secretary of State can either hold a public inquiry or allow the appeal to be heard by the Planning Inspectorate.

Powers of enforcing authority to carry out remediation

If the contaminated land needs immediate remediation, s.78N provides powers for the enforcing authority to take action and then recover costs under s.78P (not unlike powers in statutory nuisance when the LA abates the nuisance). Recovery of costs can include placing a legal charge on the land. The enforcing authority can take action:

- Where there is an immediate danger and action is needed to avoid serious harm or serious pollution of controlled waters.
- Where the 'appropriate person' makes an agreement with the enforcing agency for it to carry out the work.
- Where the enforcing agency is precluded from including something in a remediation notice under by s.78J or s.78K.
- the 'appropriate person' fails to take action
- no 'appropriate person' can be found.

Hardship provisions

Section 78H provides for situations where the 'appropriate person' is unable to pay and in some cases the local authority will bear the cost (or part of cost) of remediation if the 'appropriate person' is unable to pay. In considering undue hardship, the LA takes into account whether the costs would force a company into liquidation. Lenders (*e.g.* Banks) are only liable if they take possession of the land, see DETR Circular. Under s.78X(3), Receivers are not liable unless they take unreasonable action which causes pollution to occur.

Penalty for non-compliance with remediation notice

Under s.78M it is a criminal offence not to comply with a remediation notice unless the person has a reasonable excuse. The case is heard in the magistrates court and the penalty on conviction for contaminated land on industrial, trade or business premises is a fine not to exceeding £20,000 and a daily fine of £2000 for every day the remediation until compliance. In other cases the fine is not to exceed level 5 (£5000), and 1/10th of the fine per day until compliance. If the enforcing authority considers the summary proceedings ineffectual, it can take proceedings in the high court to secure compliance.

Public Registers

Under s.78R, information is held in public registers on land designated as being contaminated including remediation notices, remediation statements, appeals, convictions and remediation work carried out.

Future developments in contaminated land regime

Under the current s.78A(2) of the EPA 1990 even a trivial amount of polluting matter entering controlled waters is considered 'pollution of controlled waters'. The Government is adding a clause to the new Water Bill to amend s.78A(2) to make it 'significant pollution of controlled waters' and allow statutory guidance to be issued on what constitutes 'significant pollution'.

Common Law-criminal prosecution

If pollution is emitted from contaminated land and it adversely affects a number of people, the Attorney-General or LA might take a criminal prosecution for public nuisance. If a person died as a result of being exposed to contaminated land, the polluter could face manslaughter charges if grossly negligent.

Common law – civil action

Action to obtain a private remedy such as an injunction or damages.

a) **Torts-Negligence, (private) nuisance, *Rylands v Fletcher* and Trespass:** Where pollution from contaminated land has affected others who have suffered harm or loss or nuisance, there could be grounds for an action in tort, *i.e.* negligence, nuisance, *R. v F* and possibly trespass. In *Cambridge Water Co v ECL* (1994), the water company's borehole was contaminated by chemical spillages onto neighbouring land, which had seeped into the ground and had been carried to a borehole by underground water. The House of Lords allowed the appeal by ECL on the grounds that, at the time, the chemical spillages occurred, it was not reasonable or foreseeable that it would result in pollution to a borehole some distance away. The court held that foreseeability of harm of the relevant type by the defendant was a prerequisite of the recovery of damages both in nuisance and under the rule in *R. v F.* The *Cambridge Water Co* Case was applied in *Savage v Fairclough* (1999), a case involving pollution of spring water by nitrates used on a neighbouring farm. The Court of Appeal upheld that the defendant was not liable in nuisance and to be able to recover in damages, it was for the plaintiff to prove the pollution by defendant's activities was foreseeable.

b) **Contract law:** If a vendor is selling land with the knowledge that the land is contaminated, it may be sold at a reduced price on condition that the new owner indemnifies the vendor from liability from remediation of the land. Equally, a new owner may require the vendor to indemnify against future clean up costs associated with historic contamination. Following the *Cambridge Water Co* case (1994), the tannery was sold by ECL Group to the parent company, ECL Plc. At that time the NRA (now the Environment Agency) was considering taking enforcement action for remediation of the site. The ECL Group indemnified the ECL Plc against any liability for 6 years in a '*Pollution Indemnity Agreement (PIA)*'. The Environment Agency later pursued ECL Plc for remediation of the land under s.161A of the Water Resources Act 1991 a month before the PIA expired. The costs involved came to nearly £1 million and when ELC Plc tried to invoke the PIA, the ECL Group attempted to avoid liability on technicalities. The dispute was settled by the courts in *Eastern Counties Leather Plc v ECL* (2002), when the Court of Appeal upheld that ECL Plc was entitled to the benefit of the indemnity agreement.

15. EXAMS AND ASSIGNMENT TIPS

Read the exam paper carefully. Check how many questions have to be answered. If a question is in two sections, check whether either or both sections have to be answered. Check whether questions carry equal marks. Calculate how much time should be allocated for each question and when you should start each question. Beware of spending too much time on one question at the expense of others. If running over time on a question, it is better to leave some space and go back at the end if you have time.

Allow a thinking stage. Work out what the question is about. Write rough notes to help, setting out the relevant issues logically, and in order of importance.

Identify the Issues. Set out the issues involved. . .' *This question concerns the law with regard to. . .'*, but **do not** spend time writing out the all facts of the question.

State the law relevant to the issues you have identified. Give legal justifications for the statement which you have made, e.g *'The local authority may serve an abatement notice under s.79(1)(g) Environmental Protection Act 1990, if. . .'*

Apply the law which you have stated to the facts as given to the question.

Conclude your answers. The question may want you to give advice, e.g. *'I would advise the Company that if the LA finds evidence that a statutory nuisance exists under s.79(1)(g), it has a duty to serve an abatement notice..'*

Environmental law exam/assignment topics may relate to:

- A specific pollution control regime (*e.g.* comparing IPC to PPC)
- The influence of International/ EU law on a particular pollution control regime
- Planning/Environmental Impact Assessment
- Topics relating to aims of the Aarhus Convention (access to information, public participation, access to justice). Should there be an environmental court ?

- Role of Judicial Review. The influence of Human Rights Act 1998
- EU or Government policies or new proposed legislation
- Whether common law should be developed in pollution matters. Consider EU measures in relation to environmental liability
- A problem scenario

If presented with a problem scenario in exam/assignment:

1) Determine what the problem(s) is. Taking each person/company/situation at a time, work out who or what is causing the pollution and who/what is suffering from it. The victim may be the 'environment' rather than a person.

2) Establish whether the person/company causing the pollution has:

a) committed an offence. If so who will prosecute?

b) contravened conditions of a licence, e.g. IPC/PPC permit, waste management licence, discharge consents into controlled waters or sewers.

c) caused Statutory Nuisance under s.79 EPA 1990.

Section 82 EPA 1990 allows an individual to take action if LA fail to do so.

d) contravened planning permission or conditions attached to it.

3) What action can be taken by regulator ? Consider what enforcement action, including criminal prosecution, can be taken by the regulator. Are there mitigating/ aggravating circumstances which will affect sentencing. Consider what penalties can be imposed on conviction: fine and/or prison sentence, may be made to pay legal costs and/or compensation.

4) What action can individual take if the regulator fails to act?

a) private criminal prosecution can be taken by an individual in respect of any offence unless the particular Act prevents it.

b) Judicial Review. Does an individual/ organisation have standing to take a judicial review.. Human Rights Act 1998 can be considered.

c) Cost of legal action. If legal action to be taken by individual, there is the question of how it can be funded.

5) From the position of the person who has suffered harm, who are the victims and what remedy required?
Action to stop the pollution/nuisance

i) Enforcement action/criminal prosecution taken by regulator

ii) Private criminal prosecution, If regulator unwilling to act

iii) A judicial review can be taken by an individual, with standing, to challenge decision of regulator not to act. (civil law action)

b) Damages/Injunction—civil action can be taken under one or more torts, depending on the facts

- **Nuisance (nuisance)**—if proved, remedy damages and/or injunction
- *Rylands v Fletcher*—if proved, remedy damages and/ or injunction
- **Negligence**—if proved, remedy damages
- **Trespass**—if proved, remedy damages and/or injunction
- **Public Nuisance** is also a tort. Action can be taken to obtain damages if an individual has suffered over and above others

16. RESOURCES (INCLUDING WEBSITES)

University Law Libraries. University Libraries are usually open to the public to read books, law reports and journals. Availability of books can be checked through the university library catalogue, sometimes available on website. University library websites often have lists of useful websites and databases. Some electronic law journals and legal information databases can only be only accessed by subscribers. Universities may have an academic licence for particular database, allowing them to be accessed by their students. These databases often require an ATHENS password when accessed off campus.

Websites: Many government and statutory bodies now have websites, providing information ranging from policy statements to statute law/case law. Environmental Campaign groups and public interest groups often have websites. It is important to be aware that the law and/or facts on non-professional websites may not necessarily be accurate. However, they still contain very useful information and insight into the views surrounding particular issues. Some of these websites will be discontinued or relocated elsewhere. By doing keyword searches it may be possible to find a relocated or similar website.

GOVERNMENT AND STATUTORY BODIES

Gateway to UK Parliament Websites. *www.parliament.uk*
Her Majesty's Stationery Office. Includes all UK legislation. **Note:** website contains the original legislation, not amendments *www.hmso.gov.uk.*
Gateway to Government Depts. *www.ukonline.gov.uk*
Northern Ireland National Assembly *www.ni-assembly.gov.uk*
National Assembly for Wales *www.wales.gov.uk*
Scottish Government *www.scotland.gov.uk*
Dept. of Environment, Transport and Regions (until June 2001) *www.detr.gov.uk*
Dept. of Environment, Food and Rural Affairs (from June 2001) *www.defra.gov.uk*
Dept. of Transport, Local Government and Regions (June 2001-May 2002) *www.dtlr.gov.uk*
Office of Deputy Prime Minister (from May 2002) Inherits responsibilities, including planning but excluding transport or electoral issues from DTLR. *www.odpm.gov.uk www.planning.odpm.gov.uk*
Dept for Transport (as from May 2002) www.dft.gov.uk
Environment Agency(England & Wales) *www.environmentagency.gov.uk.* Click on 'news' to see details of recent prosecutions.
'Net Regs' gives lists of primary, secondary & future UK environmental legislation, designed to help small businesses. *www.environment-agency.gov.uk/netregs*
Scottish Environmental Protection Agency *www.sepa.org.uk*
Health and Safety Executive *www.hse.gov.uk*
Royal Commission on Environmental Pollution *www.rcep.org.uk*
Sentencing Advisory Panel includes guidance on environmental offences *www.sentencing-advisory-panel.gov.uk*
Magistrates Association see 'costing the earth', sentencing advice on environmental crimes *www.magistrates-association.org.uk*
Countryside Agency *www.countryside.gov.uk*
English Heritage *www.english-heritage.org.uk*
English Nature *www.english-nature.org.uk*

SUBSCRIPTION DATABASES (MAY PROVIDE SOME FREE TO ACCESS INFORMATION)

CaseTrack comprehensive database of cases *www.casetrack.com*
ENDS Report. journal on environmental policy and business. *www.ends.co.uk*
Justis database of cases, current and repealed legislation) *www.justis.com*
The Times newspaper – law reports *www.timesonline.co.uk*
Westlaw database of cases, legislation and journals *www.westlaw.co.uk*

FREE TO ACCESS DATABASES (MAY NEED TO REGISTER)

British and Irish Law Information Institute full text cases (includes high court and appeal cases). Statute law. Law Commission publications *www.bailii.org*
Court Service selected judgments since 1996 www.courtservice.gov.uk
Daily law notes important case summaries, including EJC. *www.lawreports.co.uk*
House of Lords full text judgments since 1996, find H of L, then judgments *www.parliament.uk*
Dept. for Constitutional Affairs is developing a Statute Law Database (SLD) with updated versions of all Acts, of the UK and Scottish Parliament. Will include any amendment to an Act since its enactment *www.dca.gov.uk/lawdatfr.htm*
Public Interest Lawyers some cases and materials on their environmental cases *www.publicinterestlawyers.co.uk*
Richard Buxton & Co. Public interest solicitors specialising in environmental law. free access to summaries and transcripts of their cases. *www.richardbuxton.co.uk*
Croner's environmental law and best practice *www.environment-centre.net*
Telegraph **newspaper**-law reports *www.telegraph.co.uk*

INFORMATION AND ENVIRONMENTAL ORGANISATIONS

'Guide to UK Legal System' by Law Librarian, University of Kent *www.llrx.com/features/uk2.htm*
Academic environmental law websites *www.academicinfo.net/lawenviron.html*
Country Guardian conservation group concerned about environmental damage from windfarms *www.countryguardian.co.uk*
Delia Venables useful legal articles, links *www.venables.co.uk*
Environmental Law Foundation charity providing advice on how law can help prevent environmental damage *www.elflaw.org*
Friends of the Earth *www.foe.org.uk*
Greenpeace *www.greenpeace.org.uk*
Envirowise Govt. funded environmental business programme offering advice to businesses on waste reduction *www.envirowise.gov.uk*
Letsrecycle recycling and waste management information *www.letsrecycle.com*
Mast UK organisation that helps communities and individuals with mast site problems *www.mastaction.org.uk*
Pesticide Action Network UK (PAN UK) aims include eliminating hazards of pesticides *www.pan-uk.org.uk*
Planning Sanity (includes Mast sanity) helps communities tackles adverse planning and development applications *www.planningsanity.org.uk*
Powerwatch independent organisation providing information about EMFs *www.powerwatch.org*

REVOLT campaign to help those adversely affected by powerlines *www.revolt.co.uk*
RSPB *www.rspb.org.uk*
UK Environmental Law Association *www.ukela.org*
WWF *www.wwf.org.uk*

UN AND EU

United Nations UNEP conventions, treaties, *etc. www.un.org*
European Union online *www.europa.eu.int*
European Commission – Environment *www.europa.eu.int/comm/ environment*
European Courts of Justice *www.curia.eu.int*
European Environment Agency *www.eea.eu.int*
European Environmental Law provides email update on cases *www.eel.nl*

INDEX